THE
AQUARIAN SHAMAN

"Like Star Wolf, *The Aquarian Shaman* is both a guide and a catalyst for embodying our own inner wisdom and courageous heart. We need wise elders who have been through the fires of change to hold up a light to show the way forward, and this book brings a bright, brilliant blaze."

HEATHERASH AMARA, AUTHOR OF
WARRIOR GODDESS WISDOM

"Linda Star Wolf offers teachings, insights, and techniques from her mystical and shamanic path in a generous, gentle, and accessible way. This is a useful book for anyone embarking on their own journey into the mysteries."

DANIEL PINCHBECK, AUTHOR OF
BREAKING OPEN THE HEAD

"Star Wolf's skillful approach as an Aquarian Shaman has the potential to significantly impact your life. Through her teachings, you can learn to become a bridge between the energy fields, effectively changing old patterns, thoughts, beliefs, and energy into new forms. I highly recommend this book."

ITZHAK BEERY, AUTHOR OF *THE GIFT OF SHAMANISM*

"This work truly provides a treasure map for walking the Aquarian Shamanic spiral path of transformation with which Star Wolf is intimately familiar and exceedingly adept at guiding people."

REV. STEPHANIE RED FEATHER, PH.D.,
AUTHOR OF *THE EVOLUTIONARY EMPATH*

"Linda Star Wolf gives us the incredible gift of a practical, unified, and integrated system for 'ordinary' people to access multidimensional, shamanic states of consciousness"

AZRA BERTRAND, M.D., COAUTHOR OF
WOMB AWAKENING AND *MAGDALENE MYSTERIES*

"Star Wolf has forged a powerful and carefully crafted pathway to realizing the Aquarian Shaman within. And where is the divinity contained in this brilliant journey to becoming an Aquarian Shaman? It's on every page. Take the ride."

BRIAN DELATE, AMERICAN ACTOR

"Star Wolf is a beautiful Shamanic guide who shines her light into the soul of the world. *The Aquarian Shaman* ushers in an era for evolutionary transformation."

JORGE LUIS DELGADO, AUTHOR OF *ANDEAN AWAKENING*

"This book will open new doors of perception, connecting you more deeply with inner wisdom, the wisdom of the natural world, and the wisdom of all creation."

JUDITH CORVIN-BLACKBURN, L.C.S.W., D.MIN., AUTHOR OF *ACTIVATING YOUR 5D FREQUENCY*

"You'll find wisdom contained within these words as well as practical tools to support and encourage you along the journey. This book is one of those rare gems that you will refer to for many years to come!"

STEVEN FARMER, CREATOR OF *MESSAGES FROM THE ANCESTORS ORACLE CARDS*

"Star Wolf is a force of nature who understands and articulates deep and shamanic wisdom. . . . This book is a must-read for anyone wanting the keys and tools for deep connection to their inner wisdom, purpose, and journey in their life."

NITA GAGE D.S.P.S., M.A., COAUTHOR OF *SOUL WHISPERING*

"This book leaves no stone unturned, planting the seeds to support each reader's ascension process to reveal their truest selves."

TAMMY BILLUPS, AUTHOR OF *ANIMAL SOUL CONTRACTS*

THE

AQUARIAN

SHAMAN

Walking the Spiral Path
of Transformation

LINDA STAR WOLF, PH.D., D.MIN.

Bear & Company
Rochester, Vermont

Bear & Company
One Park Street
Rochester, Vermont 05767
www.BearandCompanyBooks.com

Text stock is SFI certified

Bear & Company is a division of Inner Traditions International

Cataloging-in-Publication Data for this title is available from the Library of Congress

ISBN 978-1-59143-514-3 (print)
ISBN 978-1-59143-515-0 (ebook)

Printed and bound in the United States by Lake Book Manufacturing, LLC
The text stock is SFI certified. The Sustainable Forestry Initiative® program
promotes sustainable forest management.

10 9 8 7 6 5 4 3 2 1

Text design and layout by Kénleigh Manseau
This book was typeset in Garamond Premier Pro with Kommisar and Nunito
Sans used as display fronts

To send correspondence to the author of this book, mail a first-class letter to the
author c/o Inner Traditions • Bear & Company, One Park Street, Rochester, VT
05767, and we will forward the communication, or contact the author directly at
starwolf@shamanicbreathwork.org.

Scan the QR code and save 25% at InnerTraditions.com.
Browse over 2,000 titles on spirituality, the occult, ancient
mysteries, new science, holistic health, and natural medicine.

Honoring all Aquarian Shamans who have always existed beyond time and space.

And to Nikólaus, my beloved Aquarian Shamanic trail mate, who truly sees me and elevates our journey home to an epic adventure.

Contents

SECTION 3
THE "INNER TOOLS" TO AWAKEN THE AQUARIAN SHAMAN WITHIN

SECTION 4
SHAMANIC EXPERIENCES FOR A QUANTUM SHIFT

✳

Foreword

Lee McCormick

Life indeed moves in expansive spiraling circles and cycles. It often requires years on our soulful journey to grasp the subtleties and mysteries presented through our shared life experiences. Human consciousness is in the midst of evolution. The essence of life, and most crucially, consciousness, is transforming—unfolding and revealing itself as an integral part of the shamanic cycle of death and rebirth. I highlight this as context for the relevance of this book to our collective present. Linda Star Wolf recognizes, and I concur, that we are in the era of birthing the Aquarian light, as human consciousness expands and matures. The age of Aquarius has been foretold by both ancient and modern day astrologers around the world. It denotes an imaginary time when peace and enlightenment will finally rule our planet. And so, Star Wolf offers us her new book, *The Aquarian Shaman*, whose insights are perfectly attuned to these times.

Star Wolf is a cherished friend and Circles of Light familiar. We first encountered each other in Los Angeles in the early 2000s, where we swiftly discovered our mutual passion for the vibrancy and creativity of life, and the expansive possibilities in the healing arts. We also shared a history of recovery. This common ground formed a lasting bond between us. Some years later, I organized an event in Nashville named Circles of Light and invited Star Wolf and her husband, Brad Collins, to lead sessions. There, they taught Shamanic Breathwork and presented "Thirty Shamanic Questions," and were met with resounding success. They subsequently teamed up with me and my esteemed colleague, Joan Borysenko, Ph.D., at another Spirit Recovery event, where Star Wolf and Collins illuminated the gathering with a profound Shamanic Breathwork session and various ceremonies throughout the three-day retreat in Joshua Tree.

I entered this world on the twenty-fourth of January as the moon traced its path across my native Florida skies, continuing over my beloved Teotihuacan, Mexico, and the vibrant heart of Mexico City, where I would later begin my journey of reimagining my life from the inside out. These Aquarian times signify the return of the mystery in our consciousness. Star Wolf understands this profound truth and walks alongside the Great Mystery of life as a queen walks her realm looking out over all she sees. This is the way of the Aquarian witness— to be deeply immersed yet also cognizant that, despite our extensive knowledge and experiences, we stand on the brink of the unknown. The future pages of life's eternal unfolding remain a mystery, holding the potential for new prospects—or challenges. Our understanding is vast, but it does not blind us; instead, it propels us into the embrace of the unknown, ensuring we are vibrantly engaged with the dance of time and the Great Mystery.

Star Wolf has lived the life of a great soul on Earth. Atop a mountain, she has crafted a sanctuary, manifesting her dream of aiding those drawn to her gifts and offerings. She possesses the rare ability to bring dreams into being and sustain them in our physical realm, which is a discipline and art all its own. Taking up the mantle of her ancestral legacy, she has diligently worked to heal and liberate energies, returning them to the Great Mystery. She has given her heart wholly, and later, faced the shadow cast by the Angel of Death as her great love Brad Collins transitioned back to the spirit world. Even so, Star Wolf discovered the strength to reawaken her heart to love and partake in life's shared journey, as only a great woman can do. Yes, we men can and do love deeply, but it is the essence of the feminine soul that anchors love's depth, just as the brilliance of the Aquarian light is rooted in the heart of the feminine.

The Aquarian Shaman is more than a book; it is a beacon extended to us, inviting us to heed a wisdom keeper's guidance on a homeward journey to connect with our souls' distinctive and intrinsic gifts. This aligns with the Aquarian ethos—the journey that leads us back to the innermost spark of life, our most profound offering to this life and our world. Though we are each born from the light of creation's Great Mystery, many of us, as we mature, let go of our connection to our soul's pure light in exchange for worldly ways. We have inherited legacies full of promise and complexity, passed down through bloodlines, families, and communities—such is the fabric of our existence. Now the Aquarian age bestows upon us its gifts and entrusts us with the vital task of refocusing inward for healing and enlightenment. This marks a new and potent call of our era, and it is indeed a wondrous one!

I invite you to embrace life's challenges; to take a fresh look into your mirror, searching for your deepest self; and to affirm the potential that flickers within. We live in a remarkable era, and together we are poised to restore grace, inspiration, love, and integrity to the heart of the Great Wheel of Life. With your love and creativity, you have the power to envision and craft your life anew. May *The Aquarian Shaman* be a guidebook for your journey.

We were born for this!

All my Love,
Lee McCormick

Throughout the more than twenty years that Lee has worked in spiritual-based recovery, he has written several books and produced a documentary called

Dreaming Heaven. His passion led him to host workshops and trainings as well as facilitate groups for mental health and addictions treatment centers around the country. He cofounded the Integrative Life Center in 2010, a place where people could come to receive individualized treatment rooted in the real world. His entire life's work has been devoted to empowering people to harness the power of self-discovery and the natural world.

Acknowledgments

Once again, I offer a deep bow of gratitude to the always fabulous Inner Traditions team over the last two decades, especially to the beautiful soul who recently left this earth, Anne Dillon, who had been my editorial rock and so much more. I called upon your spirit to continue to guide me from the other side of the rainbow bridge with this co-creation that we discussed several years ago and have felt your light and great sense of humor and wisdom guiding me onward. I miss your human form but feel our soulful connection beyond space and time.

Jon Graham, words can't ever express what it means to have someone of your caliber to go to bat for me time and time again. So much gratitude to everyone at ITI for the support and faith in my creative process as I strive to communicate my soul's journey as an Aquarian Shaman and mystic over the last 40 years while serving humanity and ushering in the new aeon. Jeanie Levitan and Ehud Sperling, thank you both for keeping the faith and for your commitment to quality publishing of the wisdom teachings so needed, especially now for the epic times that were predicted by the wisdom keepers of the ages.

A special heartfelt thanks to the newer editors, Chris Cappelluti and Justine Hart, for your patience and abundant skills working with my manuscript and soul's expression in these printed words upon the page. A bow of gratitude to Manzanita Carpenter as your ongoing great work as a publicist continues onward. Many blessings to all those who work behind the scenes and thank you for doing what you do to bring more enlightenment during these powerful Shamanic times of great death and rebirth upon our beautiful home, planet Earth.

My ever grateful heart wishes to thank Elizabeth Britt for her over-the-top, stellar support as my PR person. Elizabeth keeps me on track, remembers what I forget, and shows up, come rain or shine.

Special blessings and gratitude to the countless brave, intrepid, compassionate, dedicated, planetary, visionary hearts and spirits who have been called to learn with me and my offerings through the Venus Rising Association for Transformation, who include:

* Venus Rising University graduates
* Ordained SHIP Shamanic Ministers
* Certified Shamanic Breathwork Facilitators
* Shamanic Mystery School initiates
* Transformation House graduates
* Shamanic Worldwide Mystery Tours journeyers
* Star Wolf's mentoring groups and individual mentees
* All those in archetypal, elemental, ancestral, and spirit forms, including Interstellar Guides and Guardians from the great beyond.
* And again to Nikólaus, my beloved Aquarian Shamanic trail mate with whom I dance through all the elemental worlds and beyond.

A special deep bow of appreciation to Kelley Moonwolf Eden as my sacred shamanic muse along with her amazing editorial support. I honor the deep appreciation and kinship we share for ancient wisdom as well as present day Aquarian consciousness which is emerging perfectly . . . right on time for the turning of the ages and the global shapeshifting of universal consciousness here and now on Gaia/Mother Earth.

IN APPRECIATION AND LOVE,
STAR WOLF

Back to the Future

Many years ago, I paid my first visit to the reservation that was home to my adopted Seneca Wolf Clan grandmother and spiritual teacher, Grandmother Twylah Nitsch, Yewehnode—meaning "she whose voice rides on the wind." Gram Twylah sent me out into the woods, urging me to look for what she called a "special rock person." She told me there would be a stone waiting to give me a most important message, and it was up to me to find it among the millions of rocks there. When I pressed her for more direction, she simply told me to sniff the air with my wolfy nose and follow my intuition.

According to Gram Twylah, this natural intuition resides in us all, and while we ought to first work with a teacher who can point our way, ultimately we must awaken our inner shamanic ability and reconnect to the wisdom and shamanic awareness within our own nature. She emphasized that all beings have a "shamanic birthright" and the ability to access inner truth from the sacred spirit that the Great Mystery has breathed into us. Gram Twylah believed we were entering into the prophesied times spoken of by the elders before her, and that my generation would, in her words, "witness the end of the old world and decide if there would be a new world or not for the people of this Earth." She said we were entering into the fifth world, and that the fourth world, which had come and gone before the present one, had faced great tumult and upheaval so we could all be here at this exact moment on Earth. Like the worlds of the past, we are in a period of transition, the birth of the Aquarian age. The Aquarian way is to shift from traditional hierarchical models toward the co-creative principle of shared contributions based on our unique gifts, both as individuals and groups. I call the people leading this process Aquarian Shamans.

As I followed Gram Twylah as lead Wolf Elder, over time I sensed there was an awareness within me that was continually awakening, just as she had promised. I was developing a powerful connection to the spiritual guidance I needed on my path. This was not something new or foreign, but a natural part of myself that I had left behind somewhere in childhood. I refer to this temporary loss as "soul loss." It is difficult to describe the profound joy and deep-seated fulfillment I experienced as these vital elements of my soul were restored. I began to reconnect with the magic of my true being and, in time, to share it with others. This magic, I termed my inner Aquarian Shaman, though many people have called it by different names. For me, the Aquarian Shaman is one who humbly learns from the timeless, sacred wisdom passed to them by respected elders. The true Aquarian Shaman has also learned, or remembered, how to listen to and trust their inner healer and guide, and has found a path back to wholeness. These awakening ones are driven by a profound calling to impart their wisdom to others, who may include kindred soul friends, students, or family members.

In times of old, and in a few remote villages still to this day, there exist "medicine healers," sometimes referred to as shamans. Historically, the shaman/healer or medicine man/woman was a vibrant and active member of the community who knew about healing firsthand, for oftentimes this individual had undergone a life-threatening disease, illness, or strange malady, and had found the path back to wholeness. Today, multitudes of seekers from around the world are searching out Indigenous teachers and other healers, sometimes known as shamans, in an attempt to reclaim something they intuitively sense has been lost in our modern healing methods.

Throughout the years, I too felt an inner calling and joined the ranks of hundreds of thousands of seekers. I have thus had the blessed opportunity to learn directly from authentic medicine people, gurus, mystics, visionaries, shamanic beings, and a wide variety of depth healers, sages, and teachers.

As I have now entered into my seventies on my Earth walk, I feel a renewed life force energy stirring and a deepening of my soul's path. This has infused me with a strong sense that I have been called to be here now on Earth during her great time of shape-shifting and to also join her as a force to be reckoned with. I've realized I have now become the elder I was seeking in my younger years, and while I will always be a lifelong learner, I am not necessarily looking for another external teacher—although, when we have eyes to see and ears to hear, we realize everyone and everything in nature can be our teacher. With a humble bow of respect and honor, I acknowledge all the many "great ones" I have encountered over decades, and I know I am still learning what it truly means to be a "real humane being."

As long as I have the breath of life within me, I will continue to gratefully discover new teachers and friends who have sage wisdom or advice to impart. However, some years ago, I reluctantly let go of the belief that my power lies in something or someone outside myself. While one must be careful about the shadow of spiritual arrogance, fast-food consciousness, and the feeling one has "arrived," a healthy balance is required. Anyone who has ever tackled a serious problem or challenge of any kind knows that fantasy and magical thinking are just the beginning of seeking the answers but are not the whole solution. It is best to honestly evaluate our situation and be thoughtful in our decisions and actions. Yet the challenge remains: How can we discern the next right step, or even where to begin?

Opening and surrendering to living a highly creative and magical life is different from getting trapped in fantasizing and magical thinking, or in other words, trying to simply wish such a life into being. To pass through the gateway into a magical life, one must allow sincere, conscious sacrifice and surrender of the old self by undergoing a symbolic shamanic death and rebirth. Such a life, if it is to be maintained, will require learning how to dance the spiral dance with regularity and facing the fire head-on.

A new, heightened consciousness unfolds when we focus our imagination to access inward wisdom, surrender to the inner journey, and then take action steps in the outer world to achieve what we have imagined. Simply participating in a ritual and believing the ritual alone is what effects change in your life, without actively cultivating a shift in your thoughts or behaviors, is unlikely to bring your dreams to fruition. A ritual creates a special moment for connecting with your inner wisdom, helping you to choose actions that match your goals and to let go of results beyond your control. Using the power of imagination to access our inner wisdom, which lies beyond the rigid framework of the ego mind, does not mean the world we access is imaginary. It only remains imaginary if we do not take action to manifest what we have seen or heard from our inner wisdom. Even science uses the imagination when it asks a question and inquires into the true nature of reality. Albert Einstein allegedly said, "Imagination is everything. It is the preview of life's coming attractions." Our inner world shapes much of our identity. By tapping into our imagination, we bring unconscious thoughts to light and gain insights that enable us to move beyond conventional problem-solving to discover more innovative solutions and creations.

The ego mind serves to ensure our basic needs and safety, but it can hinder us when we need creative answers. Through my introspective journey, I've learned that in these highly transformative times, we all have the capacity to awaken and embrace our inner visionary—the Aquarian Shaman—who guides us in rediscovering our authentic selves and imagining our future potential. This inner guide, deeply loving and unfailingly trustworthy, directs us toward meaningful coincidences that lead us to our true purpose. Our Aquarian Shaman embodies the collective wisdom of our ancestors, passed down not only through physical cells, but through the enduring power of our imagination, which connects us to our past and guides us to our future. This inner guide is like a time traveler, deftly navigating beyond the linear flow of time to whichever aspect of ourselves—the past, present, or future—is necessary for our current challenges and heartfelt needs. This capacity is the essence of true magic and wonder, and the best part is that it's an integral part of our very being. It is not only possible but also a crucial step on our evolutionary journey as humans.

Grandmother Twylah once said to me, "We are all native and indigenous to the sacred Mother Earth." In saying so, she was encouraging me to "step into my grounded roots," as she put it, and embrace my own shamanic/spiritual path of beauty and power, the path of my soul's death and rebirth. My journey of several decades as a sincere seeker of truth and wisdom has led me through many such deaths and rebirths. At various times, I have embodied my soul's path of planetary service in a multitude of roles, such as a mental health social worker, addictions counselor, licensed therapist, author, workshop leader, oracle reader, Shamanic teacher, midwife, minister, ritualist and channel, and Shamanic Breathwork Facilitator and Teacher. As a dedicated elder in "the sacred work," I have felt a deep desire to create safe and highly effective ways to make contact with the inner wisdom and love that is our birthright.

Looking back, it's clear that my journey toward personal healing was a destiny waiting to be fulfilled, yet this epiphany only struck me at age twenty-nine. It was a pivotal moment when I recognized the necessity of self-focus to advance on the path true to my soul. Since childhood, I had been inclined to aid in the healing of others, be they human or animal, but maturity brought the insight that sometimes one must heal oneself first to be of greater service to the world. Although I have always naturally stepped into a leadership role, much like the Alpha Wolf, in whatever situation, or role, I have entered into, I also had a shadow that I had hidden from my own consciousness. I have written about this in great depth in several of my other books so I will only mention it here briefly as it is old news in my world and to many of my readers and students. I was unconsciously medicating my emotional pain with alcohol until March 21, 1982 (forty-two years ago). Until I faced my own inner demons I was not fully in integrity with my self and others. The Shamanic path is a purifier and demands self-honesty and integrity in order to authentically transmit healing transformational energy to others.

Several decades ago, I embarked on a dual career as a certified counselor and addictions professional while also immersing myself in various forms of holistic and shamanic training. These included the emerging early schools of breathwork, musical journeys, sound healing, bodywork, expressive healing art, group dynamics processes, and deep energy work as well as Reiki. My extensive, deep journey inspired and led me to create a magical unified system of shamanic healing, which I named the Shamanic Healing Initiatory Process (SHIP), detailed in Chapter 12 of this book. Further, I studied and trained with masters and, over decades, distilled the essence of numerous breathwork methods, shamanic teachings, depth psychology, and my personal experiences into a unique and powerful transformative ceremony, the Shamanic Breathwork Process, which I developed and trademarked over thirty years ago.

The call to the Aquarian Shaman journey often arises from life's pivotal moments, be they illness, loss, or a profound desire to connect with the spirit. Once heard, it becomes an undeniable summons to self-discovery and healing. For many decades the Shamanic Breathwork Process/Ceremony has been a potent tool I offer to those on their own inner vision quest. It facilitates deep transformational healing and embraces shadow work, and the rediscovery of one's sacred purpose. This powerful shamanic ceremony employs sacred breath, chakra-attuned music, energy bodywork, artistic expression and outer processing with another as a sacred witness in order to release blockages and pave the way for communication with one's future self.

Breath is central to spiritual practices across traditions, a key to healing that's been with us from life's inception. By breathing intentionally and surrendering our monkey minds in a supportive environment, we can enter an altered state, connecting us with the powerful Aquarian Shaman within to rejuvenate our lives and realize our fullest potential. This book delves into the wisdom of giving birth to and embodying your inner shaman, providing practical tools for transformative growth and profound shifts in consciousness.

Let the great mysteries be not less magical,
but become more accessible.

Aquarian Shamanism Made Accessible

1

Why Become an Aquarian Shaman?

The shamanic path to our true selves begins with the first step and unfolds moment by moment, day by day. Embracing the Aquarian Shaman is central to my spiritual journey and my role in guiding others toward realizing their potential. With over forty years of dedication to this path, I've helped thousands of soul seekers to respond to their calling. Whether you're seeking to deepen your self-understanding or you're at the cusp of a new journey, this book offers a gateway. I invite you to join with your beautiful, open heart and mind, as well as your curiosity and creativity, to explore your dreams and purpose, and to awaken the Aquarian Shaman within as your sacred guide on life's adventure.

While many people will offer different and conflicting definitions of shamanism, to me a "shaman" is a sacred transformer—someone who discerns and alters stagnant energies or outdated beliefs to alleviate restlessness and pain. Acting as a conduit between past, present, and future energies, a shaman facilitates the metamorphosis of the old into something new, much like trees shed their leaves or snakes their skin. We, too, should embrace letting go to make way for new growth. Through continuous transformation, we can increase our capacity for joy and reduce the level of suffering necessary for awakening and positive change. As I learned from one of my dearest mentors, Seneca elder

Twylah Nitsch, we can learn from wisdom or woe; it's often preferable to foresee and avoid the pitfalls rather than repeatedly endure them. Addiction has often been defined as "doing the same old things repeatedly while expecting different results."

This book calls upon those who are ready for significant changes to explore the path of the Aquarian Shaman, a journey within everyone's reach. It's about surrendering to and embracing the mystery of life—acknowledging, as Gram Twylah used to say, that "If we knew exactly what the Great Mystery was, it could no longer be called the Great Mystery!" Aquarian Shamanism is a transformative process, a willing exploration into new realms of love and wisdom, integrating them into our daily existence. Being shamanic means allowing parts of our lives to change or fall away, sometimes abruptly, sometimes gradually, so we may live with greater meaning and purpose. With deepening truth, humility, integrity, and grace, over time we step into our soul's birthright and embodiment as Aquarian Shamans.

Regardless of whether you are at the beginning of an awakening journey, or have become adept at working with multidimensional realities, perhaps at times you still find yourself depressed. You may feel stuck, helpless, hopeless, or anxious, or you may be subject to inexplicable outbursts of rage and anger. Or perhaps you simply have an inner longing to embrace your personal power and a meaningful way of life. You may yearn to live fully in accordance with your dreams and visions, and to seek transformation, instead of settling for the temporary fixes that are ubiquitous within shallow, mainstream consciousness. These feelings have been a driving force for many spiritual seekers. Notably, over the past few decades, many people have sought a more personal spiritual connection to the divine, a direct experience rather than one mediated through a priest, spiritual director, or guru. I refer to this intimate connection with divine forces as the Spiral Path of Direct Experience, or simply the spiral path. This book will provide a treasure map for walking the Spiral Path of Direct Experience, the path of an Aquarian Shaman. Over the course of our journey together through these pages, I will suggest tools and techniques for navigating your emotions and experiences and guide you to a deeper awareness within yourself, empowering you to take decisive action in your outer world.

In the course of our human lives, we inevitably meet with challenging events that test our resilience. Often we fall back on ineffective coping strategies such as overwork, perfectionism, addictive behaviors, or simply having an obsessive desire for control. These temporary fixes eventually fail, revealing the need for new, healthier tools in our "medicine bag" to support our well-being and allow us to pursue positive change, purposeful work, and fulfilling relationships. Soul initiations, or life crises, force us to reassess our lives, our relationships, and our treatment of our bodies. By proactively choosing to engage and dance with the deepest parts of ourselves, and to step upon the shamanic spiral path of transformation, we will have put into place daily practices and skills that allow us to navigate life's difficult waters, earthquakes, fires, and winds. This inner work builds a strong self-relationship, making us our own best guides. While guidance from others can be valuable, learning to also rely on our inner Aquarian Shaman ultimately leads to choices that resonate with our deepest selves.

When we adopt daily practices that lead us to profound personal truths, we will awaken the Aquarian Shaman within. This process helps us recover parts of our being lost to trauma, so we may find joy and embrace a rich, full human experience. It is termed "soul retrieval" by some; however, many years ago I was taught by my Cherokee friend and soul sister, Teresa, to conceive of this metamorphosis as simply a deep releasing, a healing at a cellular level, and a renewal of the spirit. I now often describe this transformative work as soul return, shamanic consciousness, or soulful recovery.

Most of us bury and suppress our inner Aquarian Shaman during early childhood due to cultural conditioning. While our earliest soul loss is originally provoked by other people and by society, as we grow into adulthood our own inner guardians at the gate—our ego defenses—stand ever-vigilant for anything that threatens the ego's power over us.

Our egos employ a myriad of methods to keep us asleep, including end-less distractions of our own making. These distractions not only keep us unconscious of self-destructive behaviors, they can also keep us dulled and disconnected from pain for limited periods of time. However, these distractions soon become addictive patterns, and we need more and more of them to keep us numb, asleep, and disassociated from external reality. These addictions can remain unseen by us, and even after we awaken to them, they can feel impossible to overcome. Hopefully, one day, we become sick and tired of feeling sick and tired, and we realize we've had enough of trying to run away from discomfort and pain. At this point, the journey home can finally begin. We find the humility to admit we are feeling unfulfilled, and the courage to walk through those forbidden doors within us. Much to our amazement, we discover hidden treasures in the shadowlands of ourselves, where our lost soul fragments were safeguarded until such time as they could be reclaimed, a time when continuing to deny our true selves would create dire conse-quences. This soul surrender brings immense relief. It "hurts so good," to quote John Mellencamp, because we are breaking through denial and stepping into the light of truth, regardless of the opinions of others or the dictates of our own frightened ego.

Shamanic awakening and the continuing spiritual practice of liv-ing in daily communion with our shamanic awareness is both humbling and, at the same time, incredibly empowering. There is good reason for this dichotomy: both these feelings are true. Once we can admit we have been asleep, going through the motions of being alive, the light of consciousness can break through the cracks in our armor and begin to spread through our whole awareness. After we've awakened, it becomes difficult to go back to sleep without even more severe consequences. Our true selves remember that we are not on planet Earth by accident. If we are not here accidentally, then we must be here on purpose! Having had this revelation, we might prayerfully ask, "What is my sacred purpose?" We must then listen to what message arises from our beautiful awak-ened minds and hearts.

Everything on Earth has a connection to the Great Mystery. It is where we came from and where we shall return. During our human lives, we have made an agreement to incarnate, to become embodied spirits, and to fully remember our elemental bodies and spirits. This means that while our origins may be divine, we are intrinsically tied to the elemental forces of water, earth, fire, and air, all infused with the Great Spirit at the core of the Creator's shamanic heart. I believe the Creator has a shamanic essence, as we do, because just as children bear traits of their parents, it naturally follows that the ultimate Creator of everything has birthed all beings, and all manner of life, in its sacred image throughout the universe. This image is made up of both matter and spirit, and it is time we learned to honor both as sacred. After all, our maker sent us here not as a punishment, but as a blessing, so we could awaken spirit within the flesh-and-blood human aspects of ourselves and fulfill our destiny of becoming Aquarian Shamans, our world's Co-creators.

For a long time, many have been oblivious to their own spiritual slumber, as though an age-old enchantment had stripped us of our inborn wisdom and the divine power granted at birth by the Creator. Awakening the Aquarian Shaman within teaches us to traverse life's challenges with grace and integrity, allowing us to make choices that serve everyone's best interest, rather than reacting out of emotional impulse. Change is our inherent nature, yet sometimes, fearing the turmoil it brings, we confine ourselves to restrictive patterns for a semblance of stability. True strength lies in our power to be humble, flexible, and adaptable, continuously learning to navigate the spiral path of life, echoing the universe's own spirals, and naturally reinventing ourselves as part of the natural world.

Embracing our inner shaman leads to a symbolic death of old patterns and a rebirth into new possibilities. It is about unifying within the heart, from a place of unconditional love, the baser energetic vibrations of human experience—"I need," "I want," and "I will"—with the elevated spiritual expressions of "I speak truth," "I see truth," and "I am truth." This inner alchemy is the heart of transformation, balancing our earthly and spiritual selves. It's the work of the shaman to marry these dualities into a harmonious whole, and not deny one or the other, but instead birth within ourselves the sacred third of both/and. Engaging in this continuous transformation, we weave connection, harmony, and enchantment into all facets of existence, making the embrace of our inner Aquarian Shaman a compelling journey.

2

What Is an Aquarian Shaman?

An Aquarian Shaman is a person who has sensitivities, skills, and innate or learned abilities to access and observe the natural and supernatural worlds in order to bring into the physical realm a higher wisdom and love from a plane of existence beyond time and space. People call this plane by different names: the universe, the cosmic, God consciousness, the Great Mystery, the great beyond, or the place of Oneness, to name just a few. In essence, a shaman is one who can bridge two realities that sometimes oppose each other. The shaman, through this unique ability, can bring healing and wholeness to the core wounds of humanity, which are borne by every person on Earth. Through the ages, traditional shamans have often been referred to as "wounded healers," because they have accessed their sensitivity to human suffering through their own core wounds and have been able to recognize and bring wholeness to that core wound within themselves. In this process of returning to wholeness, a shaman gains a level of empathy and compassion that allows them to become conscious of others' core wounds and gift that consciousness to the wounded. To be an Aquarian Shaman is to be a part of the world around us and give to that world. More than a role, it is an inner calling, an empowering soul path and way of life. It's not a 9-to-5 job, or a role at a workshop, it's who you are 24/7.

Historians tell us that the word "saman," which has been translated as "shaman," came to us via Russia in the 1600s and originates from ancient Siberian peoples. Because the people of Siberia had a language that was verb based, the word "shaman" is not intended to be static, but is a vibrational word of movement and action, relating to how the energies of both the natural and supernatural worlds are flowing through someone who is recognized as a shaman or spiritual teacher. Rather than "shaman" referring to a static state, role, or title, to truly embrace the essence of the word, we ought to speak of one who is "shamaning."

The concept of shamaning emphasizes the dynamic movement of creative energy that one must dance with in order to walk between the worlds. This way of being requires a commitment to follow the spiral path of transformation and co-creation in every moment, to be deeply connected to the nature spirits, and to commune with the excited vibrations and frequencies that flow through nature. In other words, when one is able to raise their energy field into an excited vibrational state and merge with that field in sacred holy communion, they are shamaning.

Shamanism has survived for thousands of years and has shown up in similar forms in Africa, Asia, Europe, Australia, North and South America, and even on remote islands around the world. In other words, wherever you find human beings, if you search deep enough, you will discover their shamanic roots. Traditionally, a shaman is the member of a community who is known as a holy man or woman or person, who was either born knowing how to interact directly with the spiritual and natural worlds or has apprenticed over time in these ways with powerful elders. Shamans are called upon to perform a wide variety of sacred services, whether offering healing to an individual or leading traditional ceremonies for the community.

Through my extensive studies, which include Jungian depth psychology, I've also come to see that modern shamanism owes much to Carl Jung, the Swiss psychiatrist whose work in analytical psychology provided a foundational framework for these practices. His exploration of archetypes offers profound insights into the human condition, enriching the psychological and spiritual dimensions of contemporary shamanic practice. A shaman is one who can access these archetypal energies in order to bring healing to themselves or another. Thus a shaman must continually strive to become a clean and pure vessel, or "hollow bone" for these energies, so the archetypes that flow through the shaman may serve the highest good for all concerned.

Carl Jung is known for being one of the first who described the theory of synchronicity. The theory of synchronicity relates to meaningful coincidences, or events that have no apparent causal linkage, yet seem to the observer to be meaningfully connected. Grandmother Twylah taught me many years ago that there is no such thing as coincidence, only synchronicity and one's ability to follow the signs. What she meant was that if something or someone comes into your path, especially three or more times, this crossing of paths has a meaning for you—it is synchronistic. However, discerning the meaning requires an initial recognition that something of significance is speaking to you, followed by patient and attentive listening for the intended message to emerge. In other words, we live within a magnificent road map whose signs and symbols are all around us at any given moment. However, to grasp them, we must step outside our mundane daily routine—you might say we need to listen with our third ear, or see through our third eye. The meaning in these synchronistic events is ours and ours alone, although they may also carry implication for others we encounter on our path.

When we practice watching for synchronicity, it begins to show up to such a degree that we can no longer dismiss it as coincidence, and we are barely able to keep up with all the information coming to and through us. We come to sense, and eventually acknowledge, that these ostensibly random signs are an answer from the universe to a prayer that our heart's yearning sent out long ago. I have learned that this is the way the universe shows up to support me and let me know I am headed in the right direction. Through these synchronistic events, we are invited to see that we are co-creating our lives with an aspect of our wiser self, our Aquarian Shaman guide. After all, who sent out the call from deep within our souls, and who can recognize and interpret the encoded messages that return in many sacred forms, if not ourselves? As I have worked with countless soul seekers, I have observed time and again that everyone has their own inner guide, like an internal GPS system that can be directly accessed through learning how to journey to the Aquarian Shaman within and work with these signs and symbols. In my life, synchronicity abounds everywhere around me. I never take this way of life for granted; rather, when I follow this inner shamanic connection, gratitude flows through me and brings with it divine grace. One of the best ways to keep this energy flowing through my life is to be of service, and practice being a loving shamanic soul to others who are ready to awaken their own Aquarian Shaman. This has been my soul's work for many years now, and the magic and miracles it has created have exceeded my wildest prayers and dreams.

Because the language of the soul and our inner Aquarian Shaman is metaphor, imagery, and feeling, we need to be willing to "see" with new eyes, through our imagination, if we are to receive and understand the messages from beyond. The Aquarian Shaman is not confined to traditional boundaries but embraces the unity of knowledge and imagination. As we will discuss in Chapter 16, an Aquarian Shaman deftly weaves threads of scientific understanding, such as lessons learned from the journey of a caterpillar becoming a butterfly, into a rich tapestry of vision and metaphor that speaks to the soul's organic metamorphosis. As an Aquarian Shaman, the ability to work within the world of imagination, archetypes, signs, and symbolism is important, and once we learn the skills to do this, we find there is a much bigger, deeper perspective available to us all. Historically, the importance of imagination was emphasized in the art of Indigenous shamans. Pictures of animals, symbols, and shapes were drawn upon rocks to show the tribe what a shaman saw on a journey or vision quest to retrieve vital knowledge from the great beyond.

According to Grandmother Twylah, we are all spiritual beings doing our best to navigate this Earth walk while confined to our Earth suits. When we are born, we are deeply connected to our imagination and the expansive plane beyond space and time from which we have come. It is the challenges, hurts, and harsh realities of survival on Earth that cause the connection to fray. Everything in this Earth world has its counterpart in the other world, its double; as above, so below. When outer and inner are made one, we inhabit the sacred third space of shamanic consciousness. Perhaps this is what Jesus meant when he said "the kingdom of heaven is at hand," and "I and my Father are one."

To reach such a state of oneness and clarity, or shamanic consciousness, is to know and understand all parts of who we are. As William Blake wrote: "If the doors of perception were cleansed every thing would appear to man as it is, Infinite." When we have eyes to see, we begin to perceive things as they really are, in their wholeness. We realize there is no inherently good or bad part of us, but that we all possess a full spectrum of human emotions, characteristics, and experiences. Recognizing and integrating all parts of what make us human, from our divinity to our base needs, is to reconcile the opposing forces within that create duality, judgment, and shame. Through this reconciliation we can find inner harmony, which enables harmony in our external lives. Thus we begin the journey of an Aquarian Shaman.

3

How Aquarian Shamanic Techniques Serve Everyday Life

Opening our eyes wide enough to see the both/and of life, instead of having an either/or mindset about our own experiences and the world around us, gives us the perspective to see the bigger picture of life and accept that failure and loss are as much a part of our journey as victory and joy. When we gain this insight, it liberates and energizes us. However, once we "remember" this profound truth, we must learn to stay awake in an outer world that may not yet have shifted. Awakening our Aquarian Shaman requires the bravery and discipline to break free from limiting norms and embrace our true potential. Linear thinking assumes life should progress in a straight, ever-ascending line, equating deviation from this path with failure and interpreting challenges as punishment. This mindset, a remnant of patriarchal cultural norms, suggests that hard work directly leads to happiness and merit. So when life diverges from this pattern, it disrupts our ingrained beliefs, often leading us back into unhealthy perfectionism. Even today, this very obsolete thinking can still shake my world when I face hardship and disappointment.

The shamanic spiral path, a spiritual tradition I not only practice and cherish but also impart to others, honors the non-linear journey of direct experience. This way of being is much kinder and more forgiving, allowing our humanity and spirituality to have space for growth. After all, we are here on Earth to be both human and spirit and to learn to integrate both into our identity, as part of our unique sacred path.

To maintain a shamanic awakening requires daily dedication to spiritual practices that prevent relapse into destructive habits and keep us on the path of conscious awareness. Another way to conceive of this, which echoes the thinking that underlies twelve-step programs, is that before we can change a habit or behavior, we must acknowledge its existence within us. Once we can see what has been, we can put into practice new techniques and can take steps, one day at a time, to maintain a new way of being. The Big Book of Alcoholics Anonymous compares following the twelve steps to putting money in the bank. The steps, or practices, must be carried out every day, even on days when one feels good and might not feel a need to practice. In this way, one accrues reserves in the bank that can be accessed during more stressful times. An Aquarian Shaman must be able to look within and identify what no longer serves their evolution, and then use the tools they acquire, every day, to stay awake and to allow for ongoing transformation.

Yet shamanic practices reach another level beyond twelve-step program philosophies. The ceremonies and rituals we perform allow us to commune with a power higher than ourselves, through nature, the elements, ancestors, and kindred friends and family. As well, certain sacred objects can grant us wisdom, when we are open to receiving it, thus reminding us we are not alone on the journey. When we use drums, rattles, and smudge—the smoke from burning herbs used to remove negative energy—we are engaging the dynamic and creative energies of the spirit world. In this way, we raise our own vibration beyond the base motivations mentioned earlier, such as "I need," "I want," and "I will," and connect with the wisdom of the spirit realm. Having done so, we can then make use of that energy in our daily human lives. When we create art mandalas after connecting with these energies, we are accessing the language of the soul and bringing the message to a physical form through art. All these are tools of shamaning.

Shortly after my twenty-ninth birthday, during the initial cleansing of my own doors of perception, I made a commitment not to go back to sleep. Since then, I have renewed that commitment each day. As we traverse the shamanic journey where life and death intertwine, encountering old habits during times of change is natural, not a sign of failure. If we can recognize and respond to these moments with compassion rather than self-reproof, we will be able to continue along the spiral path, understanding that life's difficulties are part of the continuous cycle of nature. We can acknowledge that our relapse is simply a sign that something big is happening, and the ego defenses are signaling "red alert!"

During such times, the shaman becomes the "shape-shifter." We may need to call up the shamanic warrior within, who will motivate us to move through a challenge with greater fire and have the courage to push through to the other side. Or we may need to summon the shamanic peacemaker, who knows how to let things go; or the shamanic artist, who paints the landscapes of life anew each day; or the shamanic nurturer, who can provide gentle sustenance to us in a painful time. Or we may call upon the shamanic ceremonialist, who will use ritual to help us find meaning and closure to a difficult experience—in other words, symbolic death—or will perhaps bring recognition and celebration to an accomplishment or new circumstance—symbolic birth.

The inner Aquarian Shaman embodies traits that resonate with the sacred, ever-changing elements: Water reflects the shaman's emotional, intuitive, nurturing essence, with a flow that cleanses and dissolves. Earth signifies manifestation, practicality, fertility, abundance, and grounding. Fire represents desire, passion, sexuality, the spark of creativity, active transformation, and purification. And air encompasses the sacred breath, expansiveness, inspiration, clarity, vision of the larger picture, and rebirth. As an Aquarian Shaman, when I am fully aligned with creation, I can sense all these elements dancing in a lovely balance within my being, and I find myself intimately experiencing the Great

Spirit and Great Mystery as they orchestrate this dance of the elements through my soul. These moments of oneness are so profound that they overwhelm, inspire, and motivate me—as well as those with whom I have shared these teachings—to practice living in shamanic consciousness in everyday life, with incredible results.

Shamaning means accessing a state of excited energy, a state that is available to everyone, though some take to it more naturally than others. When children everywhere are allowed to live and learn freely from nature, they carry this imprint of shamanic wisdom close to their hearts throughout their lives. They are better able to live in natural rhythm, walking a spiral path rather than a liner path. As adults, many have left their magical childhood connection with nature behind, but it is never too late for us to re-enter the "kingdom of heaven" again, if we can reclaim our inner child from long ago. Recovering our birthright connection to nature and the divine is only a breath away.

When I awakened to this reality, I committed to birthing the Shamanic Breathwork Process that had been gestating within me for decades. Before developing Shamanic Breathwork, I facilitated other well-regarded breathwork forms for many years. Yet embodying the role of a transformer and Aquarian Shaman demanded additional effort beyond my prior training to achieve and maintain the vitalized state necessary for such work. The Shamanic Breathwork Ceremony was created by combining my own creativity with the lineages of Indigenous wisdom handed down by trusted elders, as well as ceremonial techniques, deep psychological training, music and art therapies, healing arts, theological lessons, and spiritual practices. All great teachers initially seek external knowledge for an extended period of time, but true inner awakening allows us to discover our deepest self, ensuring that we step into leading and not only following. This awakening, always accessible to all, is now being experienced by more people than ever before. The time is upon us; some may call it the age of Aquarius, or simply evolution, but regardless, it is the right timing for mass consciousness to step into the light of true being.

Over many years, my staff at the Venus Rising Association for Transformation, the shamanic nonprofit I lead, have trained thousands of students to become Aquarian Shamanic way-showers and facilitators. In this manner, the awakening of the Aquarian Shaman is carried out into the world and has the potential to reach every human and living creature on Earth. It is primarily an inner awakening, one that can create far-reaching effects on relationships to self, loved ones, purpose, and work, as well as to the Earth and the divine. We are all interconnected and interdependent, so when we do the inner work needed to awaken, embody, and transmit, we are able to be the forces of nature and change we wish to see in the world—and that is what being a shaman means to me.

Historically, small populations turned to sages or shamans for healing and guidance. As we move beyond relying solely on external authorities for answers, we're now embracing the chance to find wisdom within and assume greater personal responsibility. In order to enable a massive Aquarian consciousness shift, a great number of us must take part in this profound evolution. There are too many people on the planet to rely on a single "wise one" for divine guidance; instead, we all need to make better choices, acting for the highest good of all. While we can respectfully acknowledge the important roles played by our leaders, be they shamans, priests, doctors, midwives, or politicians, we cannot expect them to do vital healing and transformation work on our behalf, or make decisions for which we alone are responsible. We are all passengers on this great planetary SHIP called Earth, and we must do our part to set sail, discover, and co-create new maps, steering ourselves onward into the Void and the Great Mystery.

The "web" also known as the "circle of life" is now a mainstream term, made popular with the hit Disney movie, and later award-winning Broadway musical, *The Lion King*. The web of life is a field of energy that connects all life forms to one another—human, animal, plant, mineral, and spirit. Physicists describe what is called the "quantum field," the fundamental field of energy that is thought to be the basis of the universe's material reality. Quantum physics laws allow for particles to be in two different states at the same time. This concept of embodying two states simultaneously recalls a shaman in an altered state of consciousness, a walker between the worlds. Whether a person enters this dual state through Shamanic Breathwork, as I do, or through other tools and techniques such as plant medicines, lucid dreaming, or Vipassanā meditation, the goal is to awaken a part of ourselves that has been asleep, to access the one within who is dreaming our lives into being and who knows the bigger picture. Through these trancelike states, we begin to grasp the reality of our true selves as multidimensional beings, manifesting our excited creative frequencies on many levels. Thus, we each awaken our inner shaman. I cannot think of anything more exciting, and I continue to fall in love with this way of life every day.

Remembering to live my life daily in the presence of shamanic love and consciousness has given me hope when none was to be found anywhere on the external horizon. When we are able to find hope in this way, we are better able to adapt to the ever-changing landscape of life. We become more resilient, confident, and competent in handling ourselves as mature humans who treat one another and the planet humanely. Our relationships, circumstances, community, and life experiences become deeper, more sustainable, and more loving. To become an Aquarian Shaman is to bring wholeness to your life, which can positively impact those around you. In this way, practicing shamanic techniques serves everyday life.

SHAMANIC MEDICINE TOOLS AND PRACTICES

4
Lessons from Nature
Shamanic Ritual and Magic

Living magically means embracing life's bigger picture every day, a practice that transforms our reality, shifting us from seeing ourselves as victims to recognizing new, exhilarating possibilities. Often the answers and meanings we seek are not hidden but await our change in focus to become evident. I am reminded of a friend who recently took a camping trip. A rattlesnake had curled up in front of the tent, and my friend tried to point out the snake to their camping companion. But until it moved, their fellow camper couldn't see it! The snake, due to the natural camouflage pattern on its back, was hidden in plain view. Hearing this story reminded me that, at times, my own old familiar patterns of thought can blind me to what someone else may see clearly. Once I refocus my vision, I can perceive what seemingly wasn't there a moment before.

We define "magic" as mysterious or supernatural forces or powers. "Supernatural" is defined as relating to an order of existence that transcends the normal laws of nature. If magic is supernatural, and supernatural is beyond the normal laws of nature, then living a magical life is based upon embracing our "super-nature," the part of us that can learn how to dance with water, earth, fire, and air, and how to co-create with these elemental beings and with our own spirit. When we add the "super" to "nature," life takes on a magical feeling, and light surrounds what once seemed dense, dark, or even boring.

Let's take a moment to consider the magic that is already in nature. Nature is a pro at being shamanic. It constantly reflects the true nature of things to us in patterns of birth, death, and rebirth. The spiral path of seasonal death and rebirth can best be witnessed in nature. One of my favorite ways to remind myself daily of the importance of these patterns is to look to the true elders of our world: the mountains, waters, trees, plants, and animals. They are much older than human beings, and they are full of wisdom. The green nation—trees and plants—has long been a great teacher to me, especially the standing people, or trees. My husband and several of my dearest friends and colleagues are blessed to live in community at my Loveland Sanctuary Home and Venus Rising's Elemental Retreat Center in the lushness of the magical blue mountains of Western North Carolina, next door to the Cherokee Nation. As I look out over the verdant mountain forest scenery through the large windows of my octagonal home, I am in awe of the dance of life that plays out before me through all seasons. I feel an eternal gratitude for the deep kindredness I share with these magnificent beings, the mountains and trees, which are filled with so much light while deeply rooted in the earth.

There are literally millions of these standing people, the trees, breathing and mirroring back both my spirit and mortality at the same time. They are at all stages of the great cycles of birth, life, and death, with younger saplings beginning to put down solid roots as gigantic elder trees tower above them. In the summer months, I often feel I am looking out at a vast, rolling sea, with so many shades of green I didn't even know existed. And as fall arrives, the colors of the foliage become even more differentiated, with a multitude and variety of hues—yellows, oranges, reds, and even shades of purple and blue. Eventually nearly all the trees turn completely brown and release the last of the dead leaves to the winter winds. As dramatic as this display of color and change can appear to the human eye, the strong, proud trees—formerly fully adorned, now standing naked in the dark winter cold—never once believe they've done something wrong when their leaves begin to fall. I doubt any tree or bush will ever go to therapy for feeling it was their fault that they changed in this manner. Perhaps because they are much older and wiser than us, they understand it is all part of the growth process. They must release the dying leaves that no longer serve the cycle they are entering.

Nature offers thousands of such teachers. In all of nature, which includes our fellow humans, there is a reflection of ourselves looking back at ourselves. As my Mayan shaman friend Eric Gonzales says, "Hello, another myself." By adopting this perspective, we can truly see that inner and outer are one. As with the example of the trees, in the shamanic world, everything reflects a larger process at play. We ourselves are composed of the same sacred elements as nature—water, earth, fire, and air—thus we embody the spirit that drives creation's cycle, mirroring life's evolutions. Though the trees shed their leaves, which appears a kind of death, there is always a hope that enters the human heart when it remembers that, come spring, the shoots of green return, a rebirth of new growth and life. Remembering this Aquarian hologram in nature, we can embrace life's transitions with understanding, peace, and grace, guided by this natural shamanic death and renewal.

Ritual and ceremony are key ingredients to living the magical life of an Aquarian Shaman every day. We are all living ritualistic lives whether we know it consciously or not. For instance, not only obvious rituals like celebrating holidays, but also everyday tasks—including brushing our teeth, getting dressed, or going to work—can be considered ritualistic. When you add a new daily ritual such as meditation, dream journaling, deep breathing, or yoga, your whole life can change. The simple shamanic tools described in this section will help you embrace the magical in everyday life.

Finding magic, inspiration, and hope in the current landscape of cultural upheaval is absolutely vital. Divisive and polarized social and political viewpoints have most people feeling on edge, and there is a great deal of uncertainty and disorientation as a result of daily reporting of catastrophic local and world events. Everything seems more intense in our contemporary world, from overpopulation and the rise of super-viruses, contracting a severe illness, to extreme weather events related to the warming of Mother Earth and the increase of global wars and horrible violent acts, to the more personal and intimate struggles within ourselves and our personal relationships. If ever there was a time to invite love and magic into our lives, and to amplify new and better skills for navigating life's difficulties, it is now.

In the past, many humans have turned to a church or religious organization for comfort and guidance, and in fact many still do. During the early stages of awakening to my Aquarian Shamanic path, I often questioned my changing viewpoints, my old belief system, and even my earlier spiritual experiences. I saw them as "wrong," mistakes that needed to be discarded now that I had seen the "light." This thinking was not all bad, since I clearly needed to thoroughly clean my inner house and let go of self-sabotaging patterns and beliefs. However, I was still thinking linearly and throwing the baby out with the bathwater, as the saying goes. I discounted my journey's lessons, failing to see the value in blending diverse beliefs and experiences into a cohesive whole. Stuck in a rigid mindset, I believed there was only one unchanging path forward—a viewpoint I notice many still hold in the world today.

On the Spiral Path of Direct Experience, we acquire many Aquarian tools and techniques to cultivate our relationship with all that is divine. These tools and techniques are your personal "shamanic medicine chest." Like a first aid kit in your cabinet, these are the ways we can heal ourselves and our lives in a direct, personal, and self-responsible way. At the core of this medicine chest is the relationship we have with our own hearts. To become a shaman is first and foremost to humbly become a person of true and clear heart, while creating healthy, strong boundaries with that which does not "grow corn" in our lives. Learning to listen to your Aquarian Shaman within is a crucial step in the process of fully awakening and activating your shamanic heart. In subsequent chapters, we will explore shamanic tools and techniques that support our daily awareness and practice of connecting with shamanic consciousness and operating from our hearts, with examples and exercises for how to cultivate these practices in your own life.

☙❧

SHAMANIC EXERCISE
Tree "Medicine" Journey*

Take a deep breath, and find yourself in a gentle place where you will feel safe enough to release and let go of that which no longer serves you. I want to call in the energies and the wisdom of the beautiful, strong, proud trees. The trees that have been filled with green leaves on their branches, standing proudly beneath the sky and bright sun, and the fluffy clouds moving overhead. During the summer season, there's been a sense of fullness, perhaps a richness, abundance, bountiful energy, fully embodied. Really embrace yourself as this tree, in your magnificence and glory as you feel into the season as it begins to change in your life. All the signs are telling you, just like the tree leaves in the fall that begin to turn colors and gradually fall to the earth, that you are undergoing a similar process. Much like the tree, you can feel that colors are changing, that the winds are blowing and the energies around you are shape-shifting. And so now it is time for you also to begin to release and let go. Gradually if we were watching the trees in the fall, we would see the leaves begin to fall to the earth. The wind and the rain comes, it speeds up the process. It's as if our emotions, our own grief, sadness, perhaps confusion, misunderstanding, or just simply not knowing what's coming next, creates the sense of loss. We can learn from the elder trees as they stand there gracefully in the cold winds and the rain, as the season changes.

---

*If you would like to listen to this journey, I invite you to access the audio version at audio.innertraditions.com/aqusha, for a more immersive experience.

They seem somehow proud, and yet humble. As they stand there starkly naked against the fall and the winter sky. There's a certain courageousness and energy emanating from the trees and yet there doesn't seem to be a struggle.

I often feel a powerful acceptance from these mighty beings as they send their roots down more strongly into the earth and simultaneously send their branches more strongly out into the sky. They have the ability to be anchored and to let go at the same time. Perhaps you can take a deep breath now, and exhale fully, and imagine with your eyes closed, that you are that tree standing there under that brilliant blue sky, in the winter with the winds blowing, and that you too, with dignity and grace, are releasing whatever needs to be let go of at this time in your life. Trusting that it's just a season, just a cycle on the spiral path of shamanic transformation. By saying that it's just a season does not reduce the gravity or perhaps the grief or the fear, but it does create an acceptance that on the spiral path that all things must change. Change means death. But it also means re-birth. There's a promise that when we release and let go, that the season and the cycles will continue to move forward on the spiral wheel of transformation. And when it does, the sky becomes softer, the winds are warmer, the rain is gentler and we find ourselves once again sprouting our own leaves and fruits, bringing forth more creation into our lives. Slowly we notice that we've grown.

Much like the trees you watch grow each year, and see that they've grown wider and taller with roots deeper under the earth creating a huge network of connection to all the other trees in the vicinity in the great forest, we put our own roots down, there's a way in which we connect with the roots of others, especially those who are on a similar path – our kindred spirits. Taking another deep breath, and imagining now that your branches, like the trees, are now fully in bloom once again. Perhaps there are tiny acorns growing in your branches, or maybe new fruits, or hundreds of thousands of amazing multi-colored green and yellow leaves, adorning your branches. Let the wisdom of our elder brothers and sisters, the standing people, the trees, become part of our wisdom; wisdom of how to let go and to clear any time that you need to. Take a deep breath, exhale fully, and come back with a gently heartfelt gratitude and deep remembrance of the sacred spiral dance of birth, of life, of death and shamanic re-birth on the ever-winding shamanic spiral path.

5

The "Good Medicine" Chest

In the shamanic world, it is important to cultivate and create "good medicine" in all areas of your life. "Medicine" here does not necessarily mean taking a pill to make you feel better. Our personal medicine is connected to our inner shamanic voice that guides us toward our personal power and spiritual healing gifts. As children, we were very close and connected to our true essence, and we knew how to "play" into many aspects of ourselves. We were natural shape-shifters, saying to one another, "Hey, let's play like you're Batman and I'm Robin!" or "I'll be the daddy and you be the mommy!" or "I'll be the prince and you be the princess!" This is a natural part of childhood; in our curiosity and creative genius, we act out many different future selves that we can imagine and embody, and in this way, we have our first experiences with archetypes. There are certain characteristics and behavioral patterns in Batman, Robin, mommy, daddy, prince, and princess. When we "try on" these character suits, though we don't know it as children, we're playing with archetypes to get a feel for our possible future selves.

In childhood, our play was a form of ceremony. Perhaps we played "tea party" and sat around a table with one embodied friend and several other "imaginary friends," to create a ceremony for gathering and communion. Most children have some form of toy box or treasure chest full of tools that allow them to try on imagined selves, like outward shamanic costumes and tools. Likewise, many children have a small box tucked in the closet or under the bed where they collect gifts and trinkets from special friends, and items of sentimental value found on escapades through parks, woodlands, or the backyard—in other words, sacred objects. We are born with the capacity to live an imaginative life in which we can shape-shift based on our dreams and circumstances. Creating our adult shamanic medicine chest is an invitation to return to that childlike wonder and curiosity, while bringing adult wisdom and intention to the process, so that what is imagined can be brought fully to our embodied, flesh-and-bones life. In this way, we can effectively use our skill of imagination to manifest real, actionable change, rather than getting stuck in a dream world to escape reality.

Playing with or working with the shamanic tools in the medicine chest is a daily practice of asking ourselves, "What do I want to play with? With whom do I wish to play? What do I need to cultivate in my life? And who do I want to be?" When we bring these questions to the altar of our lives as a daily practice, we bring purposeful intention to our play. We can open to all possibilities of life, recapturing our child-like, curious "beginner's mind," and trusting that what we are envisioning and working with is a real personification of co-creative energy, shared between our embodied human form and our higher knowing at a soul level.

Connecting to our Aquarian Shaman within can become a light-filled, joyful process, building profound self-trust and insight into life's journey. This inner depth becomes our wellspring of resilience, allowing us to access the Aquarian Shaman's tools in our spiritual medicine chest to creatively overcome challenges and emerge into higher expressions of our purpose. Our resourcefulness also comes from the friends we meet on the shamanic path who are willing to play and live in this way, who can speak our creative language and serve as a vibrant, wholesome, and motivational mirror to us, accompanying us on life's shared journey.

To cultivate good medicine is to allow for your inner guidance to be passed through an open heart from your soul essence. Your shamanic medicine chest is quite different from the medicine chest located in your bathroom at home, although at times you may choose to use one over the other. As you begin to discover your own healing energies, you will find yourself drawn by your inner shaman to a path of healing and transformation. These shamanic energies will also pull you toward outer medicine teachings, sacred objects, and shamanic tools that will resonate with the power, magic, and mystery within you.

When I teach others to create their medicine chest, I enjoy the play on words. I see the human body's chest as the physical form that holds and supports breathing and sacred breath as well as the healing power of the human heart. The heart is the energetic connector between the upper and lower energy centers, known as chakras in Hinduism and Buddhism, and the place where love is born and is felt most powerfully. Recently, modern medicine has found neurons in the heart, which indicates that not all thinking is done in the brain. The human heart, in addition to its other functions, possesses a heart-brain composed of about 40,000 neurons that can sense, feel, learn, and remember. The heart-brain sends messages to the head-brain about how the body feels and more. So, activating the heart with the breath is the key foundation to a strong medicine chest.

Until the 1990s, scientists assumed that only the brain sent information and issued commands to the heart, but now we know information is transmitted in both directions. In fact, the heart-brain is a complex, intrinsic nervous system, a network of several types of neurons, neurotransmitters, proteins, and support cells, much like those found in the brain proper. Perhaps when wise spiritual teachers have advised us to listen to our hearts and not only our heads, this is what they meant. When the chest and heart are wide open, healing energies can flow. As stated by the HeartMath Institute, "When the physiological coherence mode is driven by a positive psychological state, we call it psychophysiological coherence." This flow of energies between our psychology and physiology is a personal, coherent resonance, a synchronization of the body, mind, and emotions. The relative synchrony of these systems can be measured by our heart-rhythm patterns. The more balanced and smooth the patterns are, the more in sync, or coherent, we are. At such times of wellness, we may find our heart medicine more easily and accept it as truly our own. Creating your personal "good medicine" chest, then, is first and foremost about building a right relationship with yourself and aligning your actions with your grounded, open, and balanced heart.

SHAMANIC EXERCISE
Medicine Chest Journey*

This ceremony is to support you in opening your heart, and embracing the good medicine that's deep within your own chest. In the shamanic world, it's important to create the good medicine in every area of our lives. This medicine is not necessarily about taking a pill or something from the outer world, but it's more about the condition of what I refer to as your medicine chest, or your heart-mind. It's been said in the Bible that as a man thinketh within his heart, so shall it come to pass or so shall it be. It's important to remember that what we hold closest to our hearts, closest to our heart-mind if you will, will surely come to pass as we ruminate about it, meditate upon it, dream about it, envision it. There's a communication between our brain and our heart and the deep union between the two.

So, this is where I want to invite you to place your hand upon your chest. This is where the strongest medicine in all of your life resides. Feel the beating, like the drum, writing your own medicine chest in your own heart. With each beat, you can feel the drum within you, opening your heart, taking you deeper into an altered state, into an expanded state where you can move past what I would

---

*If you would like to listen to this journey, I invite you to access the audio version at audio.innertraditions.com/aqusha, for a more immersive experience.

call sometimes, the lesser things, or the lesser gods, and move in to what's real and authentic for you. So, take a deep breath into your heart, feeling it beat like a drum, know that this is where your true strength, your deepest intuition, your deepest heart's longing, resides. This is where your medicine will take root, and grow in the world if you're able to connect your heart to your thoughts, your feelings, and the rest of your body.

Imagine, with your hand upon your heart, that you have an inner eye—some call it the single eye—from your third eye, that can peer all the way down into your chest cavity, and into your beautiful, vibrant, healthy passionate, open heart. Just concentrate for a moment with your hand on your heart, to feel that powerful life force energy. Take a breath, and exhale fully. Giving your heart more of what it needs, sacred breath. Taking in the precious air, the oxygen, comes to us from nature itself. The exhalation of the trees is the inhalation into our hearts. Trees are such powerful metaphors for sending us their breath, an exchange between us. Breathing in to the lungs, which often times has been compared to the images of trees. It's as if we have trees surrounding our heart, on the inside of our chest. Our lungs. Filling your whole chest up again, exhale fully. And expand your heart. In that expansion, take a moment to envision the true medicine that lives within you. What's in your medicine chest? What brings you inspiration? What guides you through your own dark nights of the soul? Are you weary, lost, tired, disappointed, confused, frustrated, and even angry? If you can take it into your heart and breathe, there's the possibility of a transmutation. The medicine in your heart can heal the ills of the world that you have taken on.

Again, as a man or a woman, what we think with our heart shall come to pass, and so we want our thoughts that we meditate upon repeatedly, not to be unconscious ones, ruminating, going into places of victimhood, or constant anger, or a certain frustration, we want to become conscious of what we're thinking and the messages that we're sending into our medicine chest. The heart will bring about what we focus upon. So, take a moment to breathe into your heart. And exhale. Several times. Clearing out the heart and the chest. Cleansing that area, and replacing it now with the truth of what you truly desire, with your full faith that you have the ability to heal yourself, to transform your life, to bring healing transformation to others. That you can share your medicine chest with others and even teach them how to breathe into their hearts, release their own traumas, open their hearts again, remember their innocence and trust, and to renew faith, love, and inner knowing and wisdom. This is the most powerful medicine and medicine chest available to us. While we may have medicine chests in our bathrooms that hold different medicines that help if we get a scratch or headache or fever, some things can only be healed and transformed by the medicine within our own hearts. Taking another deep breath now, sending back out into the world your breath, riding upon your breath, is your heartfelt intentions for your deepest desires for yourself, for those you love, and for the world itself. And when you're ready, take another deep breath, exhale fully, and thank your heart. Perhaps you place your hand on your heart, and give it a massage in a circular motion. Or pat your heart. Or face your face down towards your heart and speak gently to it. Saying, thank you. Thank you. Thank you.

6

The Power of Coming Together in Sacred Circles

A community circle can be created whenever two or more are gathered, and can allow space for finding common ground and connection. Sacred circles might take the form of knitting groups, book clubs, or meetups for hobbyists of all kinds. They can also be a place where people come together to study a new skill or craft, such as divination cards, astrology, dream circles, meditation, cacao ceremonies, or festivals for ecstatic dancing. They might mean a simple walk in nature together, during which people discuss what is observed or felt along the walk. They can be lighthearted and playful gatherings, or they can be created with an explicit intention for personal growth, as with a twelve-step meeting, meditation group, or priest/priestess circle. Underlying any type of circle is the intention to come together face to face, eye to eye, and heart to heart for a shared purpose.

Many years ago, when I was sitting in a circle at a Native American gathering of wisdom keepers, I was handed a small wooden stick that had animal carvings, feathers, and small crystal stones attached to it with leather straps. Grandmother Twylah Nitsch passed this "talking stick" to me and invited me to share my "sacred point of view."

She explained to newcomers that the talking stick was being passed so each person sitting in the circle could share what was of concern to them, and asked that we share truthfully what was in our hearts and minds. She reminded each of us that we were to share something about our own personal situation or journey, and to avoid gossiping or personal attacks. Whatever we shared—be it happy, angry, sad, or confused—was our sacred point of view from where we sat on the medicine wheel of life during this moment. She also asked us to keep an open mind and heart as we spoke and listened, and to practice non-judgment of ourselves and others. Grandmother Twylah said that speaking in this manner, with no fear of being judged, would allow us to listen and speak from our innermost being, thus enabling a sacred witnessing. Deep spiritual inner healing could arise from this sacred witnessing, bringing change to our outer lives as well. When we are held in the open hearts and minds of others without judgment, everyone is transformed by the experience. She explained that since we all bear wounds from imperfect upbringings, we each have our own perspective, and our insights reflect where we are on the path of healing. Active listening—without trying to fix or judge—fosters deeper compassion for both the speaker and ourselves, revealing our shared human struggles and diminishing the isolation in our suffering. Wouldn't it be wonderful if this Aquarian Shamanic medicine became the way of the world, of governments, organizations, communities, and relationships everywhere?

Throughout the years, I have sat in many such circles and have frequently hosted them myself. They can only work if those who attend aren't trying to always be right, or control what others say or think. The group members cannot give advice or feel invested in being seen as better. Nothing creates a sense of deeper understanding and belonging than a circle that promotes sharing in this manner. Often when we open our minds and hearts to what others have to share, individuals feel their unasked questions are answered, and new perspectives come forth.

ೋಲ

Host an Aquarian Sacred Circle

Early on in my shamanic experiences, I felt called to create sacred women's circles. While I was initially driven to do so by a need within myself, in hosting the circles, I found they also helped and supported others. In this next exercise I invite you to consider what sort of community or connection your heart is seeking at this time. Do you desire a lighthearted regular meetup over a cup of tea? Or do you wish to broaden your knowledge or skill in a craft and to share in that learning with others? Are you looking to start a walking group to enjoy nature? Perhaps a men's or women's group is calling to you, or a parents' and children's group to support kids in learning shamanic communication. Or maybe you want to overcome negative habits or addictions in your life, and you wish to establish a shamanic twelve-step program to support yourself and others—for those in such a situation, I have included as an appendix to this book the Twelve Steps of Shamanic Recovery and Discovery, which I co-created many years ago with friends and colleagues.

For our next exercise, I urge you to let your Aquarian Shamanic soul be your copilot, and ask yourself, "What is it that I most yearn for and also wish to share with others?" It may take some courage to put your idea out there, but you might start with just one other person, if it feels more comfortable. The two of you may, in time, choose to bring together a wider community. Your sacred circle might take the simple form of learning to use a talking stick to encourage respectful, active listening between yourself and a significant other, child, or friend. The rewards can be rich when we begin connecting to others with intentionality.

If you feel called to host a larger circle, you can assign a topic of focus, or open the circle with a reading from your favorite spiritual teacher and allow sharing around the circle to happen organically.

Pass the talking stick or object around, or place it in the center after each person shares, and let people choose when they are ready to participate. It may be beneficial to open the hosting of the circle to other group members and alternate who offers a reading or opens the circle in their own way. Circles can happen daily, monthly, annually, or whenever the call arises within the group. A circle can also be held with friends or family to facilitate a difficult discussion or make decisions based on group consensus. I urge you to experiment with this powerful way of gathering and communicating. Tap into your heart's desire for connectedness, and let creativity and imagination support you in creating circles of communion and shared experience.

7

The Energy in Sacred Objects

Collecting objects for objects' sake is not the shamanic way. It is the meaning we find in an object, and the ability to hear the message in that object, that gives it spiritual power. Ideally these sacred items come to us by synchronistic means, whether from nature, wisdomkeepers and elders, soul companions we meet on the journey, or animals we have connected with in some way, such as finding a bird feather on a forest path. However, because potentially sacred objects from all over the world are now seen on the shelves of New Age stores, it is important to acknowledge that the sacredness of an object always comes from our own connection with it, the way it speaks to some inner part of ourselves, whether we discover it on a hike through the forest or pick it up off a dusty, forgotten shelf in the back of a shop. Often a sacred object then becomes a part of our altar or has a place to hold in a ceremony or ritual.

Many years ago, I learned from my Native American teachers that you can be sure something is your medicine when it calls to your heart at least three times in a row over a short period. Three is often the number of manifestation, and if you listen and receive whatever is showing up in your sacred space three times, it will gladly reveal its secrets to you. You must pay attention and honor it, for everything shines when it is loved, as I know from my own experience. Now that I have shared the story of the talking stick circle with Grandmother Twylah, it is relevant to share how my first talking stick came to me, as an example of how to see and hear in a new way as you bring sacred objects into your life.

Many decades ago, after a very emotional Integrative Breathwork workshop that I attended in Dahlonega, Georgia with my breathing teacher Jacquelyn Small, I walked outside into nature and literally stumbled over a small stick. I bent down to pick it up, as I had now learned the importance of stopping and taking another look at objects or experiences that showed up on my path. It was an unusual stick, six or seven inches in length and three or four inches in diameter, with dark carvings made by insects in the wooden stem. It was smooth and pleasant to hold, since it had lost some of its outer bark. About three-quarters of the way to the top of the stick was a wooden growth, bulging out with what is referred to as a burl. Burls on a tree occur as the result of the tree trying to wall off and protect itself from some sort of stress, injury, or pathogen. This is a good metaphor for how humans, too, wall off their stresses and hurts as a way of protecting themselves.

At the time, however, this particular stick appealed to me not for any rational reason, but out of a deeper instinct. So I picked it up and took it home, where I began to decorate it with stones, feathers, and leather strings tied to small, charm-like figures. I even added a few drops of my own blood when I cut my finger by accident, and felt I could share a part of myself with the stick. Soon I began sitting in nature with my stick and asking it questions, learning to listen quietly for its answers, which came to me like an inner voice. After getting to know my stick, I decided to share it with others. At the time, I was working as a mental health and addictions counselor in the small town in Western Kentucky where I grew up, and needless to say, in the 1980s in this region, the idea of a sacred stick did not go over well with some people. Yet I knew that the "sacred medicine ways" I was learning, or remembering, were equally if not more healing than the traditional therapy techniques I used in my counseling practice. I had a burning desire to share this sacred medicine with others, so I began to hold talking-stick circles inside the traditional mental health system, on the sly, as well as independently in an office I rented where I could teach breathwork and other cathartic shamanic tools. It wasn't long before my groups were overflowing, even in this town that was predominantly fundamentalist in its religions and held a limited worldview. I found a following of individuals who felt stifled by the repressive energies holding the old patriarchal forces in place. They were hungry for shamanic soul circles and the healing power of the breath that revealed their inner truth. I helped people to radically shift their lives for the better, yet while this change was deeply gratifying for me on many levels, I also faced repercussions at my place of employment. I was advised to stop using unorthodox therapies and spirituality in my groups.

Soon after, I made the decision to take what was, for me, a giant leap of faith, and leave behind the so-called acceptable, medical mental health and addictions methods of healing, so as to follow my heart's inner knowing and enter fully onto the path I still follow today. This was more than thirty years ago, and I can honestly say I have never once looked back with regret. The talking stick truly spoke to me, and my inner shaman heard its call and answered.

When you begin to observe and bring into your life your own sacred objects, be patient, and listen quietly and carefully for what kind of medicine they are offering you. It is a daily practice to learn to listen for that small inner voice that whispers an object's message. The object speaks to a part of you that is beyond your thinking mind, and so one must still the thinking mind in order to truly hear. Even the way an object looks can carry meaning; for example, a stone might appear heart-shaped or have a "face" in it that speaks to you. Or, as in the doctrine of signatures of plants, the surface of a leaf might contain a shape that is symbolic for you, relating to some part of your body that needs healing. You might have learned in a book that a crystal has a certain quality of healing energy, and you may feel a need for that energy in your life. If you have gathered the information from a book or teacher, let yourself "feel into" that object more deeply for the personal message it has for you, beyond any text or teaching. Sacred objects are sacred because they touch you in a meaningful way and help you remember your deep elemental connection to them; they are messengers assisting you in entering into the greater story of your life.

SHAMANIC EXERCISE
Find and Create Your Personal Talking Stick

If you are feeling inspired—or "in-spirited"—to find or be found by your own talking stick, one of the best ways to call your personal talking stick to you is, of course, to go for a walk among the trees. Allow plenty of time so you will not feel hurried and can enjoy the beauty that surrounds you. Try not to have too much of an agenda, and trust that if you are feeling called to connect with a talking stick, then perhaps it means the talking stick is calling you and your paths will surely cross. As you walk, feel your feet connect to the earth beneath you with gentle reverence—you may even decide to remove your shoes! Clear your mind slowly and easily by taking deep breaths and exhaling fully. Pay attention to gentle inner nudges or strong attractions you might feel to turns in the path, until you arrive at the place you feel you need to be. You might then look around and pick up sticks that catch your eye. Your talking stick may not be the first one you pick up; sometimes we need to sift and sort to find what is ours, while at other times we stumble on the perfect thing by accident—in other words, through synchronicity. Whether you find your stick immediately or need to look a little longer, you will know when you have found it. It will be the one that most attracts you, even if at first you do not know why. It will speak to you within your own mind and heart—no, you aren't crazy, sticks do speak! All of nature talks to us if we have the ears to hear and the heart to listen.

Once you have your stick, if you choose to, you may sit with it in nature for a while and get to know it in its natural surroundings. Perhaps you will spot the tree you think it came from. Whenever I remove something from where I found it in the natural world, I first ask for its permission, and then I leave an offering for the spirits of the earth. It can be a very modest offering, such as a hair from your head. One traditional Native American offering is a pinch of natural tobacco or cornmeal. I also say a simple prayer, but even simply to say "Thank you" is fine. Once you have returned home with your stick, you may wish to decorate it right away or wait until a later time when you have become more familiar with its frequencies and energies. If you listen closely, it will tell you if and how it wishes to be decorated and what kind of energy it carries. Possibly you'll begin to feel a bond and friendship with the spirit(s) that lives within your talking stick. You can rest assured the conversations between you will never be dull or boring!

Always treat your talking stick with respect, and perhaps give it a special shelf or a cloth to wrap it in. You may wish to clear its energy from time to time using the smudging method. Smudging employs fire and burning of plant material to elementally purify an object or space. It is usually done by lighting a candle and then burning a cleansing incense or dried herbs such as sage, eucalyptus, or cedar. You can perform smudging for your stick while offering prayers from your heart. Eventually, if you choose, the talking stick can be shared with others during various kinds of gatherings. During our Venus Rising training groups, we always pass a sacred item symbolizing the talking stick, so each person knows they have everyone's attention when they share their words.

By hearing the talking stick call to you, you are on your way to learning how to humbly listen with your higher heart-brain and signaling to the universe that you are an Aquarian Shaman.

8

Altars as Portals of Communion

My relationship with altars has varied and changed throughout my lifetime, because they are an external symbol of my search for the divine both within and without. Altars serve as access portals to a direct relationship with the sacred on our spiritual path. They also offer a daily reminder in our physical space to take time to pause and reflect upon what is sacred to us, to ask for spiritual guidance and help, and to give thanks for that guidance. Altars can be small, as when they are placed in churches or in a special area of a room or garden, or they can be very large, as with an outdoor medicine wheel or labyrinth. All these are ways of creating a sacred space and portal for a powerful direct experience of the divine.

In Latin, *altus* means "high," and *altare* means "high altar" or "high place." Early historical altars were often located on mounds, hilltops, or elevated platforms. *Adolere* in Latin means "to worship" or "to honor with a sacrifice," and in more ancient times, such as in the early chapters of the Christian Bible, animal sacrifices were burned as an offering on an altar to the God of the Hebrew scriptures.

Altars have been found all around the world and in every culture. They have long been seen as a sacred portal between humans and the divine, a place where people could focus their intentions to pray, meditate, chant, enter into ecstatic states, make offerings to their ancestor spirits, or connect with spiritual energies and deities. Altars have also been called sacred communion tables, where those we love from the other side come to us as ancestor spirits to support us on our human journeys. The Q'ero people of the Andes, an Indigenous people descended from the ancient Incans, understand an altar as a portal to the heavenly realms. The altar is, for the Q'ero, a focal point where a column of light emanates from the heavens downward into the center of Mother Earth, enabled by prayer and intention to honor the ancestors, elementals, and spirit helpers. This column of light is called a *canali* and acts as a gateway through which angels, guides, and masters from the heavenly realms may enter your place of prayer and ceremony, carrying blessings from the supernatural world.

Altars can be created by placing food, candles, incense, herbs, hair, or seeds as offerings to the spiritual realm. They can display pictures of loved ones, symbols, or words expressing prayers or intentions we hold for ourselves and for the world. Sacred objects, figurines of deities, and symbols of meaning can be used to create altars. Sometimes divining cards, runes, or other spiritual guidance tools will be placed on altars. Fresh flowers and fruit may be placed as appealing and sweet offerings to the divine. Altars can be very personal, or they may be shared with others. For instance, lovers might wish to create a relationship altar. Altars can honor a sick family member, or they can be built by a community for a collective purpose or celebration such as a wedding ceremony or sacred holiday. Constructing an altar is one way to build a connection with the divine and invite spiritual energies into your life, home, and community. It reinforces your intention to embrace peace, serenity, conscious awareness, and love within your space. I always place a candle at the center of my altar—for me, the bright, burning flame represents eternal light in the darkness and symbolizes the Great Mystery itself.

Sometimes altars are only temporary, such as building an altar for a day on the beach from objects found in nature. Others are intended for long-term use and are found in sacred temples worldwide for the manifestation of prayers. There are traveling altars, workshop altars, seasonal altars, as well as more permanent altars, all of which are inspired by both the human heart and the heart of the Great Mystery. Whatever your reason for creating your personal or collective altar, you will want to show your respect and honor it by keeping it clean and fresh and ensuring it is visited often.

For me, having a "working altar" close by is important because it is where I do crucial inner journey work and pay visits to the shamanic realms to find and maintain balance in my life. Transformation is an inside job and finds its way into our outer lives through the portals we create in sincere, heartfelt ceremony and ritual.

An altar can also be a place where difficult feelings, challenging relationships, or hurtful habits are consciously "sacrificed." We may recognize that an obstacle we are facing feels too big for us to take on by ourselves, and thus we surrender it to the altar, to be transmuted for the highest good. In this way, the daily practice of working with an altar supports our efforts to tune in to and refine our connection with the divine shamanic consciousness, and the longing in our hearts and souls that our wishes be recognized. This gives us an opportunity each day to transform any energy that needs to be shifted in order to maintain clarity with ourselves and our lives.

Another soul-nourishing way to create an altar is to plant a garden around your home or in a community space. It can be a large garden or just a few potted plants, figurines, and sacred objects on a patio. With this type of altar, you can play with how to represent each of nature's elements—water, earth, fire, and air—in your garden. A garden naturally lends itself to signifying the earth element; in addition, for water, you could have birdbaths for collecting rainwater, or small vessels where animals can come to drink. You might have a firepit or small chiminea, or if fire is dangerous in your region, a few solar lights could suffice. Wind chimes may be used to bring in the air element. You might learn about the properties and elemental nature of herbal plants and cultivate them consciously to represent the elements. Statues and figurines representing deities, divine guides, creature teachers, or land guardians can be placed in auspicious ways. In your garden you may have a version of a medicine wheel, or you could create a physical spiral pathway. A garden as an altar provides a place to work with the elements of nature, creature teachers, and the gifts of the earth in a practical yet creative and magical way. The transformation that occurs in a garden through the seasons is a brilliant showcase of how life progresses on the spiral path, and thus can be an amazing teacher to us.

There are endless possibilities for creativity as you give birth to your sacred altar spaces. In the end it is simply about creating relationships with the divine, with the web of life, with the seen and unseen elements that support us, and with ourselves. No matter how you are called to engage this creative, ancient shamanic practice of altar work, the altar will anchor your deepest prayers, bridging Earth and heaven and all dimensions in between. Your life will be blessed as the altar becomes your cherished companion.

ॐ

SHAMANIC EXERCISE
Create Your Personal Altar

First you must decide your intention for your sacred altar, and where you would like to build it. Do you wish to have it in a prominent space in your home, where you will see it regularly and be reminded to take time for prayer and meditation? Or is it a more private altar for your eyes only? If so, consider building it within a cabinet that can be easily opened and closed, so it is waiting for you when you are ready for silent meditation and contemplation. It could be a more social altar displayed with family photos and a candle that, when lit, sends good wishes and prayers to your loved ones. Traditional seasonal altars are often built to celebrate sacred holidays and times of year that are meaningful to you and your family. At such times, you may unwrap and place family ornaments and decorations on a fireplace altar, tree, or table. At the heart of every altar is gratitude and a longing for connection to what we love, and to the divine.

Once you have decided where to place your altar and what its intention will be, it is time to ceremonially cleanse the energetic space. There are many ways to prepare the physical space before arranging your altar items. Elemental clearing or smudging is often used and is a traditional shamanic way to engage the nature spirits to bless and create sacred space. Palo Santo wood sticks have become popular with spiritual seekers who have participated in sacred plant spirit ceremonies with Amazonian shamans; the rising smoke of the lit sticks or herbs is believed to enter the energy field of the participants and ritual space to clear negativity. Its use dates back to the Inca era. Whatever smudging techniques or tools you select, cleanse your altar space with an open heart and mind, and with joyful gratitude, sending a message to the spirit world that you are preparing a space for sacred communion between yourself and the interdimensional realm of spirit.

The next step to creating your personal altar is to select the sacred items to be placed there. The first item I choose is the altar cloth, which will be the foundation for the sacred space and objects. I have several special cloths with different images, colors, and textures, which I have gathered from many places around the world on my Shamanic Mystery Tours. I keep these cloths in my large wooden "medicine cabinet" where I store many of my sacred shamanic objects and tools. What you place upon your altar is personal and depends on what kind of altar you feel called to create. Select items that resonate with you, or with which you desire to forge a deeper bond. You might also consider placing symbolic images or inscribed notes on your altar, representing what you aim to let go of, like a smoking addiction or feelings of resentment.

In choosing your sacred items, you might select objects related to a particular spiritual or religious path; for example, Indigenous belief systems (such as Native American), Buddhism, Hinduism, Judaism, Christianity, Islam, Taoism, Goddess worship, Pagan spiritualities, Celtic Druid traditions, or any other spiritual path you wish to connect with. Be reverent yet spontaneous and playful, and listen to your intuition regarding what you want to place upon your sacred altar. Remember, your altar can be a beautiful, inviting, healing space and is a reflection of yourself, so feel free to include whatever calls to you.

After selecting your sacred objects, begin to arrange them on your altar guided by your inner awareness. Start with items you're drawn to, setting them aside as you look deeper for further inspiration. The choices may not always seem logical, but might often be a mix of deliberate intentions and unexpected spiritual nudges.

Make it part of your routine to spend time with your altar daily. Begin your mornings by connecting with it: Ignite the candle, burn some smudge, and waft the sage smoke around yourself in all four cardinal directions, then above and below, and finally draw it to your heart. Purify your altar with smoke and greet the spirits. Embrace the simple, powerful prayer Grandmother Twylah instilled in me, repeating three times, "Help!" and "Thank you!"

You may wish to sit at your altar and ask questions using divination tools, such as oracle decks, tarot cards, or runes. When you pull a card or rune, you can leave it on the altar as a reminder throughout the day that it is speaking to you and sending you messages, connecting you to your inner guide and Aquarian Shaman. Your physical altar will help your inner shaman stay awake, and thus it will create a growing connection to this wise one within. Let the sacred energy you've cultivated serve as a reminder of your highest spiritual intentions, marking the start and finish of each blessed day on this wondrous planet Earth.

9

Totem Animals as Teachers

Engaging with totem animals offers a profound and delightful means to discern the signals of our surroundings and nature, with our first experiences often being childhood pets like dogs, cats, or birds. Our frequent interactions with these companions can be part of our "good medicine." For example, I have bustling days filled with calls, writing, leading workshops, and managing the pioneering Venus Rising Shamanic Psycho-Spiritual University, as well as my personal life and family ties. Yet for over seventeen years, my late feline companion Princess Lakshmi often reminded me to pause amidst it all, insisting on my attention as part of her loving duty. She would step across my computer, sit in my lap, or even hiss at me if I tried to get on with the activities of life without first nurturing and petting her, and in the process receiving for myself a little downtime and rest. My dogs, on the other hand, consistently urge me away from routine day-to-day tasks, reminding me to walk with them in nature! In short, the animals with whom we share our lives often serve as our personal totem animals.

Grandmother Twylah called totem animals the "creature teachers." Every animal, through its unique and collective behaviors, mirrors aspects of our humanity, helping us to either nurture those qualities or achieve balance within ourselves. Another way you will hear this described in shamanic circles is that you are working with that animal's "medicine"—or wisdom and knowledge—and that by showing up to you, it has shared its medicine with you. No totem animal is of more or less importance than another. Although it is not uncommon to wish for a totem animal that seems sexy and exciting like a tiger, eagle, or snake, even smaller animals carry powerful medicine. For example, one of my recent workshop participants described her experience of "becoming the lowly earthworm." Now an ordained shamanic minister, she shares the poignant story, below, about her profound connection with this totem animal during a Shamanic Breathwork journey. The experience occurred at a weekend Shamanic Healing Initiatory Process (SHIP), where she aimed to commune with her inner spiritual guides.

The Earthworm Story

BY SUZANNE, WHITE BUFFALO HEART

I am at my fourth initiation with the SHIP program. Today's initiation was called "Embracing the Divine Beloved." I am sitting in sacred space with other co-journeyers and have listened to the beautiful teachings of Linda Star Wolf. I am ready to experience and open up to my own divinity. I am also willing to fall in love. I am ready for the process to begin.

As I take a deep breath in and exhale the breath out, the Shamanic Breathwork begins and I feel the music filling my body; my mind surrenders to the altered state, letting go of the ego mind. It only takes a few breaths before I feel myself falling into the Great Mystery of my soul. I fall into a time and place I've visited before. It's not a place of beauty, love, or peace; it is a time of cruelty, hate, and great sadness. I have experienced this time and place in many of my past breathwork sessions.

Breathing deeply in and out, I keep tumbling downward into this other lifetime, this place of fear and death. Every time this storyline comes up, I am reminded I have a sacred contract with another soul. I know this time and place needs to be healed for my own soul. So here I am again in sacred process.

I am at the site of a mass grave. It is a killing pit of genocide. Hundreds of people were shot, pushed into the open pit, burned, and buried. This is where the soul, Sheronda, was killed. I think to myself, "Have I not worked on this enough? Why am I here yet again?"

As I breathe in and out once more, the sacred music pulsates through my body. I feel my form shape-shifting. I now lie face down on the floor. I squirm and my mouth contorts as if I'm eating something. "Oh, my," I think, "of all animals to help me, it's a lowly earthworm!" I surrender. I am now the earthworm, wriggling in the dirt and eating the soil. I'm consuming what remains of the burial pit—dry bones, decay, rot. As I eat in my earthworm form, I am aware of my body processing the dirt and excreting waste into the soil, leaving nutrients behind. I keep working, eating, aerating, and secreting. I am transforming this burial site. I continue working until the ground turns into beautiful, sacred new earth. Earthworm's work is finished! Earthworm lays on top of the earth, exhausted from his endeavors, and surrenders to the element of air.

First, Red Robin comes, the songbird of spring. He picks up the worm and flies away. Red-Tail Hawk, the bird of higher heights, comes and takes Earthworm from Red Robin. Earthworm leaves his terrestrial home, and as he is carried away by the birds, the negative energy of cruelty, hate, and sadness is lifted from the earth. Earthworm carries with him Sheronda's soul. Sheronda has been liberated from her hell.

As I take a deep breath in and exhale out, I gaze at the regenerated earth that the humble worm has transformed. I stand now as myself, in my divine love, on sacred ground. I look around—the sun is rising in the east; it is a splendid new day.

The meadow lark calls to me, saying I am beautiful. I kneel on the earth and smell and feel the richness of the nutrient-dense soil. Tears fall to the ground, and I cry out to Earthworm and give thanks for his medicine of love. For I know my soul is renewed, all because of the mighty transformative and regenerative work of the tiny worm.

Six months have elapsed since this Shamanic Breathwork initiation experience. I continue to feel the transformation of the great mystical medicine of the earthworm. I have taken the spiral path, and with the worm's help, I have moved into a more expanded level of awareness. I wake up each morning and place my feet on the ground, feeling the safety of the earth. I am in love with this new earth. I know life will ascend to the next spiral path, but I pray I will always remember the love and medicine of Earthworm.

As another example, if you encounter a skunk as a totem animal, whether in a journey or through animal card divination, you might initially feel a negative reaction to this animal. Yet skunk medicine imparts a vital lesson on establishing robust personal boundaries. This is "good medicine" to have in our medicine chest, as boundaries are what allow us to engage in the world fully and without reservation, because we can trust ourselves to create healthy boundaries that will keep us emotionally and physically safe. If we are working with issues of codependency, the skunk is a true gift as an animal ally.

Animal totems can offer wisdom during mundane and sacred moments alike. Imagine that you are pondering how you might afford to attend a workshop or take a vacation, and suddenly, as if answering your thoughts, a squirrel appears on your fence. This moment invites you to embrace the magic and synchronicity of nature. As you observe the squirrel, consider the animal's message by reflecting on its symbolism—which you might look up in a book—or simply studying its actions for insight. In the squirrel example, a squirrel brings us the message that it is important to store up our nuts so we can have nourishment during winter. Thus, the squirrel might be advising you to practice frugality and save your money.

Over the course of your life and evolution, many different animals may be part of your "animal medicine." Oftentimes a single animal may appear to you repeatedly at the beginning of a shamanic journey. This could be your power animal or spirit guide; in other words, an animal whose characteristics you share and with which you have a spiritual bond. In many shamanic traditions, a tribe or community of people had a shared animal totem because they all held a bond with that spirit animal. For example, Grandmother Twylah Nitsch was the Seneca elder of the Wolf Clan. The wolf is also my totem, and is a totem for many who are called to work deeply with my lineage teachings. While a person can have many animal allies and totems, there is usually one predominant animal totem who will guide you throughout your lifetime. In my book *The Spirit of the Wolf,* I go into great detail about the wolf as a powerful way-showing and path-finding animal totem.

ॐ

SHAMANIC EXERCISE

Journey to Meet a Spirit Animal Guide

For this practice, settle into a comfortable seated or reclined position. Shamanic drumming can profoundly enhance the experience. With a wealth of shamanic drumming available online, you can take time to explore and select a rhythm that resonates with you. Typically I opt for a drumming session that lasts around thirty minutes. The session usually starts with a heartbeat-like rhythm, signaling the commencement of your journey. The tempo accelerates, guiding you through the exploration, and as the journey concludes, the beat decelerates to a normal heartbeat pace, cueing you to collect the insights received and gently return to your physical awareness.

Begin in your sacred space, at your altar. Consider drawing a card or placing a rune as you did during the altar's creation, to discern any guidance for your journey. Connect with the energies of your altar, close your eyes, and with a heartfelt intention or prayer, invite support from all who love you, expressing gratitude for any presence that heeds your call. Lighting a candle and using incense, herbs, or wood to perform smudging can beautifully purify the space for your spiritual voyage.

After selecting your drumming track, settle onto a mat or blanket near your altar, prepared especially for this journey. Close your eyes and take several deep, cleansing breaths. As you exhale fully, release tension from your body, and let go of to-do lists or other distracting thoughts in your mind. Then as you inhale deeply, breathe in life and vitality. With every inhale, imagine the breath is taking your consciousness down into your heart, and feel how this shift in consciousness allows for deeper relaxation. From your prepared position, set the intention to meet your spirit animal on this journey, then activate the chosen drumming track to guide you.

As the drumming commences, imagine a place in nature that feels comfortable, inviting, or even familiar. It could be a meadow, a mountaintop, or a tree or large rock that speaks to you. You might find yourself lying by a lake or river, or you may be drawn upward into the sky. Wherever you find yourself, imagine this place contains a portal through which you enter to begin your journey. Perhaps the portal hides beneath a large rock, or is activated as you dive into the waters, or by entering a cloud in the sky. As you crawl, swim, or fly through this portal, let it take you on your journey—deep into the ground or waters, or high into the skies. Become aware of any other presence you feel alongside you. Your animal spirit guide may connect with you early on, but if not, remind your inner shaman of the intention of this journey by asking it to reveal your spirit animal. You may encounter several different animals on this journey, but there will be one you feel especially called to, which you might begin to follow. This may be your animal totem. When you meet this animal spirit guide, remember to thank them for showing up. Request from your spirit guide any insights you need regarding your current life situation, or ask a question you seek guidance on. Then ease into the journey, allowing your animal spirit guide to lead as revelations naturally emerge.

As the drumbeat slows, it's time to collect the impactful messages and visions from your spiritual travels. Express gratitude to your animal guide with an imagined offering—a morsel, a sacred item, a strand of hair, or a flower or seed. This exchange fosters a balanced relationship of mutual support, symbolizing that you and your guide are in this together, on a united path of shared appreciation.

When you emerge from your journey, allow yourself to rest in contemplation and integration. It can be valuable, once you feel ready, to journal or create artwork to bring the messages you received more fully into physical reality through words, painted or colored images, or clay-sculpted shapes and symbols.

Regular journeying will enhance your connection with your spirit guide, facilitating quicker and easier encounters, even outside of meditation. As you nurture this relationship over time, guidance and support may come to you in everyday life. Like a muscle strengthened by exercise, your intuition can grow through consistent practice, making you more receptive to guidance at all times, whether during routine tasks or moments of contemplation. The shamanic consciousness thus becomes part of your day-to-day existence, so you will no longer experience such encounters as mysterious or outside the norm, but rather as comfortable and familiar.

10

Working with the Medicine Wheel

Integrating the Elements and Directions

Since childhood, I have always felt a strong spiritual connection to the natural world, and as a young adult I sought out Native American teachers, which eventually led me to my Wolf Clan Grandmother, Twylah Nitsch. She became my most important shamanic spiritual teacher. This wise elder, who carried a powerful lineage of wisdom teachings to thousands of people around the world, instructed me to always honor the elements and sacred directions. She taught me to place at least one item on my altars that would represent each of the sacred elements of water, earth, fire, and air, as well as the fifth element of ether, or spirit. This fifth element represents the Great Within, the part of ourselves connecting us to the Great Mystery that animates all life forms. It also connects us to our Vibral Core, the central locus of our shamanic power. As well, the elements of water, earth, fire, and air represent the four cardinal directions of west, north, south, and east on planet Earth.

In Mesoamerica and North America, a number of traditional Indigenous cosmologies include four cardinal directions and a center—symbolizing the Great Within. Some may also include "above" and "below" as directions—or spirit and matter—and therefore focus on a cosmology of seven directions. Each direction may be associated with a color, which can vary widely between nations, but which is usually one of the basic colors found in nature and natural pigments, such as black, red, white, or yellow, with occasional appearances of blue, green, or other hues. In some cases, as with many of the Puebloan people, the four named directions are not north, south, east, and west but are the four intermediate directions associated with the places of sunrise and sunset at the winter and summer solstices. There can be great variety in color symbolism, even among cultures that are close neighbors geographically.

Although there are many traditions and ways to honor the elements and directions, of most importance is the recognition of our connection with the elemental energies and directions, which are an outer-world representation of the qualities and characteristics we possess and utilize in our inner-world experience. We can learn a lot by watching how nature balances and works with her elements, in order to better understand how to balance and work with our own inner watery, earthy, fiery, and airy qualities. One way in which Aquarian Shamans work with the elements and directions is through medicine wheels.

A medicine wheel personifies the sacred earth. It's a haven for solitary reflection or collective rites, uniting with nature's forces, elementals, and spiritual teachers. This wheel embodies healing, balance, and transformation—the essence of the personal "medicine" we seek. It venerates ancestral wisdom, preserved in shamanic traditions, while drawing upon cosmic energies of our "future ancestors." These are the evolved echoes of ourselves, the yet-unborn facets of our soul, revealing that we are, indeed, the harbingers of our own destiny.

Creating and working with a medicine wheel is an integrative way to make use of many of the outer-world shamanic tools I have mentioned thus far—gathering in community, creating sacred altars, cultivating relationship with the spirit world and totem animals, communing with ancestors, and working with the directions and the elements. The terms "medicine wheel" or "circle of stones" have been used by many

Indigenous cultures who live close to the natural world. A medicine wheel, in its essence, is a metaphor for the cycles of life and death and the rhythms of nature, and can represent all the many stages of personal development and evolution we find ourselves in on the spiraling wheel of life. The medicine wheel most often is a physical space designed in nature and created using stones of varying sizes and shapes laid out in a circle, with special stones to mark the four compass directions. Laying out stones in this way creates hallowed ground for ceremony and ritual, both of which give meaning to the struggles of life known in shamanic consciousness as life's "initiations." When we can view our life transitions not as punishments, but rather as initiations that allow us to grow into the next octave of our personal soul evolution, we can find wisdom rather than woe from such circumstances. We can honor that struggle more easily when there is a physical place like a medicine wheel where we find the natural cycles of life reflected back to us.

The medicine wheel can be not just a physical space, but a place you carry in your mind and your way of being. It can be drawn upon a piece of paper, tattooed on your body, embroidered onto a cloth, or carved into wood, to keep with you for those times when you feel a need to work with the energies of life's cycles but are unable to visit a physical medicine wheel out in nature. Alternatively, a miniature medicine wheel can be created when you are traveling, by carrying with you a bundle of pebbles that can be laid out on a table.

There are many ways medicine wheels are constructed and utilized, but the four directions are usually represented in some way on a medicine wheel. For example: The east stone can represent the element of air, the direction of the rising sun, the season of spring, and preparing for rebirth and new beginnings. The south stone might represent the element of fire, the season of summer, youthful enthusiasm, and shadow lessons learned along the way to becoming an adult. The west stone might represent the water element and the season of fall, a time of facing our inner shadows and preparing for deep rest and even hibernation. And the north stone might represent the earth element and the season of winter, a place of connection to ancestral wisdom buried deep beneath the earth and the snow, which we receive before the next turn of the wheel, toward the east and rebirth.

Grandmother Twylah taught me that at the heart of the medicine wheel, we must place the Creator stone, a sacred point from which we invoke the Great Within. Just as my teachers spoke to me of the Great Above, a realm of celestial beings, and the Great Below, which touches the soul and belly of Mother Earth, the Great Within is where we connect more deeply to our inner shaman. The Creator stone aligns our spirit with the wheel's essence during prayer and ceremony. Thus, the wheel serves as a tangible guide reflecting our life's journey, offering a shamanic map to skillfully navigate life's transitions.

Various Indigenous cultures craft medicine wheels in their own distinct forms, each with its unique design and components. From my perspective as an Aquarian Shaman, I embrace the millennia-old wisdom of these sacred circles and acknowledge the diversity evident in their composition. There is no one correct way to build a medicine wheel. Much like an altar, the medicine wheel is a co-creative experience between you and the archetypes and spirits working with you.

I have participated in formal wheel gatherings that follow traditional protocols from different schools of thought, such as granting particular meanings to the four directions, as well as associating the wheel with specific colors, animals, herbs, and other spiritual symbols. I was also taught directly by Grandmother Twylah Nitsch how to create my own personal medicine wheel. Below, I describe just one way to understand and work with a basic and powerful seven-stone—or "stone people"—medicine wheel.

Creating the Seven-Stone Aquarian Shamanic Medicine Wheel

The seven-stone medicine wheel is a simple yet powerful layout. It consists of the Creator stone, four sacred directional stones, and one "above" and one "below" stone. I like to choose the Creator stone first since it represents and holds the sacred energies for the whole wheel. For me it is connected to my own center of power at my Vibral Core.

Moving clockwise, select the east stone, symbolizing dawn and fresh starts. It's the realm of aerial creatures like hawks and eagles, who command expansive views from above, inspiring us to embrace the open air and the morning's yellow light. They urge us to look skyward, to breathe in expansiveness, and to seek a fresh perspective whenever we crave renewal.

Next is the south stone, representing the noonday sun, the vibrancy of red, and our full commitment to life's path. It symbolizes a space of courage and resolve, urging us to embrace the sacred fires of transformation. When I arrive at this place on the wheel, I call on both the wolf and its counterpart the coyote, one representing light, the other shadow, so I can face my fears and walk bravely into my heart's truth.

Next is the west stone, the place of the setting sun, the color black, and the dissolution of old ways of being that no longer serve us. Here I embrace a symbolic, shamanic death as I walk beside the black bear into its bear cave. In this space of darkness, one truly learns how to intuitively see the whole, and be reborn in the sacred waters.

The north stone follows, signifying wisdom and love of the ancestors, represented by the color white and the midnight sun. The old ones, be they humans, animals, plants, minerals, star beings, or those who have always been in spirit form, are called upon to assist us as the next generation of wisdomkeepers and sacred ancestors on our Earth walk. It is here we acknowledge that we are the ones we have been waiting for. We become willing to step into our Earth suits as fully realized human beings, the embodiment of the teachings we've learned on our journey around the wheel, which we will share with others. Here, we show gratitude to those who came before and acknowledge their bones upon which we stand. I see the Great White Buffalo, White Owl, White Wolf, White Lion, and other elder star beings who have incarnated to become elders on Mother Earth as the guardians of the wisdom of the North direction.

I finish by adding the Great Above stone and the Great Below stone. The Great Above stone is placed outside the circle, slightly behind the north stone, and the Great Below stone is likewise placed outside the circle, slightly below and behind the south stone. This placement designates the Great Above as the locus of the Great Star Nations that connect Earthlings to their ancient kindred, star sisters and brothers from other worlds, the galactic energies, angels, and all who watch over us from the extraterrestrial and spirit worlds. Similarly, the stones' positioning represents the Great Below as the place of Earth in all its creative glory, encompassing the energies of Mother Gaia, Father Green Man, and the vast realm of earth spirits, elementals, fairies, devas, and mythological beings. As above, so below. As within, so without.

SHAMANIC EXERCISE
Working with a Seven-Stone Medicine Wheel

If you resonate with this seven-stone medicine wheel, you may wish to build one for yourself. After collecting your seven stones, go to the sacred place that has been designated for the placement of these "stone people" and arrange them in the manner I have described, either on the earth or on a cloth that is of significance to you. Choose stones for the directions of center, east, south, west, north, above, and below.

Once each stone has been placed in its proper alignment, you can put herbs in a vessel for smudging, often sage or cedar. For my herb vessel I use an abalone shell that I found on the coast of Northern California during a vision quest. I burn the herbs to honor and purify each "stone person." I have several feathers and wings that have come to me by natural means during my time as a shamanic teacher. What feather I use to disperse the smudging smoke depends on the occasion and the guidance received from my inner shaman. For instance, the wild turkey represents the good medicine of giving planetary service to humankind, so I often use a turkey wing gifted to me many years ago. Maybe you will use a feather you have found in the woods or along the beach. You can also use your hand to wave the smoke over your shell or bowl. Remember, of greatest importance during any ceremony are not the specific mechanics of it, but rather your open heart and mindful intention.

I personally choose to begin by performing smudging on myself, waving the lit smudge smoke over and around my body, front and back, above my head and under my feet, before bringing it back to my heart—imagine taking a bath in smoke instead of water. Then, starting in the center, I smudge the stones in the same order that I placed them around the wheel, letting the smoke waft gently over each stone. When I engage with the stones, I feel their spirits stir, priming themselves for ceremony. They seem eager to absorb my prayers—a crucial aspect of their hallowed role. Their joy in providing support and wisdom to humanity and all receptive beings is palpable and profound. As I smudge each stone, I say, "Welcome, Grandmother. Welcome, Grandfather." I often add, "I love you." Once I have established a connection with the sacred stones, I sit with them. Sometimes I journey by breathing, drumming, and rattling; other times I sit in silence, simply breathing and journeying, listening deeply to whatever knowledge arises. I encourage you to do the same.

You will sense when the spirits are finished speaking and the ceremony is ending, much as you feel when a conversation is coming to a close during a phone call. When you sense the ceremony's end, whether moments or hours have passed, express your heartfelt gratitude. Leave an offering if you feel inspired to—a pinch of Native American tobacco, a sprinkle of cornmeal, a strand of your hair, or anything else that intuition suggests. This is a good time to journal or draw, or create a sacred object such as a talking stick, while calling upon the guidance of your journey with the medicine wheel.

After you have worked with your seven-stone wheel, consider incorporating additional stones, respecting the diverse global traditions that link sacred wheels with celestial bodies like the sun, moon, stars, and constellations. As you explore medicine wheels, which vary in form and historical tradition, seek spiritual permission and possibly a teacher to guide your practice in a way that resonates with you.

☙❧

ADDITIONAL SHAMANIC EXERCISE
Dream into Your Own Medicine Wheel Design for Personal Healing

I urge students to heed their inner shaman, melding external teachings with direct spiritual insights. Trust shamanic practices and tools that resonate with you, whether that means quiet communion with nature, stirring music, or rhythmic drumming. As you prepare to journey inward, keep a notebook close by where you can record your visions through writing and drawing. Now close your eyes and breathe deeply in and out, until you are no longer thinking of breathing. Ask your inner Aquarian Shaman for a vision or message as to what your medicine wheel will look like, and pay attention to the messages that spontaneously appear in your awareness. Don't try to force anything, just allow and trust what comes, even if it doesn't make sense at first. Continue to breathe and follow your journey until you feel complete. After breathing for a few more moments, open your eyes. Remain in an altered state while picking up your journal or drawing pad, and let the words and images flow onto paper to describe your medicine wheel vision.

I have been blessed to participate in many medicine wheel ceremonies, and I have helped build several medicine wheels around the world. My connection to each wheel has been of significance for my shamanic/ spiritual awakening and has given me "good medicine" experiences to guide me on my way.

Forty years ago, I never imagined that my simple longing to visit a medicine wheel would give rise to the opportunity to create one myself. Such is the way of the spiral path. We begin by envisioning our heart's desire and our future self, and then, through synchronicity and love, we co-create with the conspiring universal forces to make it manifest. Often our dream is much bigger in reality than we ever could have imagined or brought forth by ourselves.

In the enchanting blue mountains of Western North Carolina, the land cradles the Star Medicine Wheel on Dove Mountain—a creation that stands as the pinnacle of my collaborative efforts, deeply connected to me in body, heart, and soul. Born from a vision, this sacred wheel marks the lands held in divine guardianship by the Venus Rising Association for Transformation. Here, retreats and workshops thrive, enveloped by the mountain's mystical embrace.

In 2003, seeking a tranquil sanctuary for sacred ceremonies and teachings, my late husband, Brad Collins, and I left the San Francisco Bay Area. Guided by a vision I had in 2001, we were drawn to find "our land," a place where we could hold trainings, workshops, and celebratory gatherings in harmony with the earth. A series of synchronistic signs led us to make our home alongside a cove nestled in the heart of the mountains connected to Cherokee land. The forty-acre tract of land we chose encompassed richly forested mountains that surrounded the cove, with a spring-fed creek gently winding through the land and emptying itself into the nearby Tuckasegee River, whose name means "crawling turtle" in the Cherokee language.

The land itself carried a healing vibrational frequency, and all who came to visit were touched immediately by the spirits of this place, so much so that several people purchased some of the land from us and built their homes in our little oasis. Shortly after we arrived to live on this land, I had another vision, which revealed to me that the Great Egyptian, Goddess Mother Isis, known by many as the Great Mother of Us All, was the main guardian spirit of the mountains and surrounding land. In acknowledgment of our guardian spirit, we named the original community Isis Cove, which honored and thrived for fourteen years before another shamanic death and rebirth took place after the passing of my husband in 2014. Gratefully, the regenerative beautiful Goddess Isis has had another plan and has been a powerful force for rebirth on Dove Mountain with the birthing of the Elemental Temples and Loveland Home Sanctuary. There are many miraculous Shamanic stories to be told about those early years at Isis Cove and how it became a place of great healing for people from all over the world through Venus Rising's workshops and gatherings, but these will need to wait for another time.

The great Spiral Wheel turned and a neighboring parcel of land became available and was threatened with clear-cutting. I was determined to protect it. Despite the financial stretch, I was armed with good credit and unused credit cards, and so my late husband, Brad, and I managed to purchase the land, becoming the dedicated stewards of what is now our cherished Dove Mountain.

Shortly after acquiring this land, I felt called to undertake a vision quest using Shamanic Breathwork to speak with the local spirits. During my breathing journey, a tiger/lion-looking creature appeared as my animal guide, and then I felt myself shape-shift into the form of Goddess Sekhmet the powerful Egyptian Lioness. My lioness self sauntered down to the stream at Isis Cove to drink the fresh water. There, I had a disturbing vision where I saw all the waters of the world becoming contaminated and undrinkable. I saw all forests being destroyed and the blue skies covered in darkness. I vacillated between fear, sadness, rage, and confusion, and didn't know what to do. I wanted to strike out at the world in terror and anger—yet suddenly I was lifted up and out of the chaos by an enormous, magnificent being, whose vast size left me powerless to fight its hold. So I surrendered and looked up into the beneficent face of the Great Mother Goddess Isis, who compassionately smiled down upon me. As I struggled, she held on firmly and calmed me by stroking me and offering these words: "Fear not, for that which is created from love will last forever." She then commanded, "Build the temples and they will come." I had no idea what temples she meant. Seeing my confusion, she spoke again: "Build the Elemental Temples of water, earth, fire, air, and spirit on this sacred land, and they will come." Great Goddess Mother Isis then showed me the unfolding of the forces of nature that would create the Elemental Temples on the land, with both large and small groups of all kinds of people sharing in sacred ceremonies around a great medicine wheel. Above the wheel sat a spirit deck where we could connect with the Great Star Nations. Isis said to me, "Begin by creating the Elemental Temples of earth and spirit, and continue from there."

I emerged from the vision shaken and overwhelmed. How could I possibly build what had been asked of me? But I began to feel more grounded after sharing the instructions I'd been given with my husband, who reassured me that we would find a way.

A couple days after this vision, a dear elder and medicine-woman friend of mine, Wind Daughter, unexpectedly telephoned to ask if I would like to build a medicine wheel on my land. Tears of joy and relief flowed down my cheeks as I shared my vision from Isis with her. Wind Daughter had built and visited countless medicine wheels across the United States. For many years she carried the mantle of medicine chief for the Bear Tribe Medicine Society, founded by the late Sun Bear, a Chippewa medicine man who helped resurrect the teachings of the medicine wheel in the 1970s, before his passing in 1992. Sun Bear was responsible for sharing these teachings with many Indigenous and non-Indigenous people, at a time when doing so was extremely unpopular and even dangerous. In addition to bringing his medicine ways to thousands of knowledge seekers around the world, he wrote several books on the subject and inspired hundreds of his followers to write their own shamanic books centering around his spiritual teachings. When Wind Daughter called, I knew the world of spirit was moving quickly, and something bigger than me had a plan. All I had to do was listen, and take action when the time was right.

A few months later, on a windy but sunny day in November, my son, Casey Piscitelli, built a beautiful, breathtaking spirit deck on top of Dove Mountain overlooking the future Elemental Temples, while thirty-seven stones were chosen for our Star Medicine Wheel.

Usually thirty-five or thirty-six stones would be used to build this type of wheel, but because of my vision of Isis, the thirty-seventh stone was added as the Isis Star Stone. Each ancestor stone was carefully put in place by a forklift, because the stones that were gifted to us each weighed about 2000 pounds. When I first laid eyes on these huge stones and heard they were abandoned and left over from blasting at a nearby quarry site, I had my doubts. But as I sought guidance from my inner knowing, I knew these gentle giants—or Grandmothers and Grandfathers, as they are often called—were absolutely perfect. After all, shamans are sometimes referred to as "wounded healers," and these stone people had found their way home to be reunited after being ripped away from their original solid block of stone. They were now thirty-seven individuated, perfect shamanic teachers on Dove Mountain, where they would bring their healing medicine and wisdom to all who found their way to this sacred site in years to come.

The Star Medicine Wheel has become an Aquarian Wheel and now plays host to a multitude of spiritual ceremonies, including memorials for loved ones who have passed, wedding celebrations, vision quests, Shamanic Breathwork journeys, healing and drumming circles, Wolf Clan gatherings, pipe ceremonies, coming-of-age ceremonies, crone ceremonies, and more recently, a total solar eclipse gathering.

At the inauguration of the Star Medicine Wheel, Wind Daughter was joined by Sun Bear's gifted apprentice, Page Bryant—an esteemed mystic, psychic, and shamanic teacher. She arrived with her beloved medicine partner and husband Scott. Many Venus Rising students and friends gathered to dress in authentic medicine wheel costumes handed down from Sun Bear's gatherings. On the morning of the gathering, before everyone arrived, we discovered one extra-large bear paw print in the damp earth next to the Creator stone. It remains a mystery how a bear walked through the wheel before the gathering and left only one paw print. Some say it was a spirit bear, others say it was Sun Bear playing a trick on us from the other side and making his approval and presence known.

We smudged to purify the space and our own energy fields, then called upon the directions, danced, and sang to the grandmother and grandfather stones, welcoming them home and calling them to wake up to receive our love and gratitude. We asked them to protect and bring healing visions to all who visited here. At the end of a very long day of ceremony, as a few of us were finishing up with a silent pipe ritual, someone suddenly said, "Look up!" There in the sky, circling above us, was a large bald eagle with a fish in its talons. We all spontaneously let out a long, loud wolf howl and watched in amazement as the eagle flew heavenward and disappeared into the clouds. Just another miracle to end a perfect day spent awakening our Aquarian Medicine Wheel with shamanic kindred spirits.

This medicine wheel was created to be a place of community and healing. It is so much bigger and more meaningful than anything I could have dreamed up on my own. For me this story speaks volumes on the teaching that no matter what the original size or shape of your dreams, when it is a personal calling to something meaningful, what begins as a simple drawing on a napkin can manifest as a seemingly impossible, great creation here on Earth and in this life. Because one of my big dreams is the ongoing co-creation of Aquarian community all over the world, my hope is that one day, you might feel called to our Aquarian Star Medicine Wheel and its teachings, and visit us on this magical land to receive its wisdom and initiation.

In this section of the book, I have laid the groundwork for some of the many shamanic tools and techniques that can be used in the outer, physical world to support what is ultimately an inner process—gaining the knowledge and courage to embrace the shamanic initiation that is enabled by difficult times. The challenges we face are designed just for us, to support us in birthing the next, higher level of our Aquarian being. In the next section, we will explore the "inner-world" shamanic tools and techniques that guide our personal healer and wisdomkeeper, our Aquarian Shaman within.

The "Inner Tools" to Awaken the Aquarian Shaman Within

11
Outer Teachings Become Inner Tools

The Importance of Imagination

> *Imagination is more important than knowledge. For knowledge is limited, whereas imagination embraces the entire world, stimulating progress, giving birth to evolution.*
>
> ALBERT EINSTEIN

If we cannot imagine it, we cannot manifest it. Without the ability to imagine and consciously create our future selves now, we only have the past as a reference point for creating our current moment. The past is largely composed of experiences, both positive and negative, locked in a feedback loop of lineage and ancestral messaging. Placing our focus on the past keeps us stuck in outworn habits and patterns, and without using imagination to envision ourselves as individuated and unique people who each have our own expression to bring forward, we will only ever be what our history told us we needed to be to survive, rather than who we're truly here to be.

Evolution will eventually bring another form of ourselves to the future regardless, without our even knowing it, but if we can flip the switch and align with our imagination, and therefore our higher consciousness, we will have a more aware, empowered, and accelerated experience of bringing our future selves to the present. Evolution takes millions of years, but we cannot wait for evolution; the survival of our planet and our species depends upon humanity bringing a more conscientious version of itself to the present time, and that begins with each of us doing our part to accelerate that mass shift.

Making these conscious, proactive, and inclusive human and planetary changes now will serve us well. With our collective imagination, we can envision the brave new world and also see our part in creating that world. Spiritual *involution*—the way we imagine and then change by bringing our future, wiser selves through our current human form—is as important as *evolution*, the process by which outer reality and landscapes change. To be *in-spirited* by a vision of our collective experience speeds up our evolution. Involution is to be *in-volved* (engaged in your inner life), *in-lightened* (illuminated from within), *in-livened* (carrying life and vitality into our human form), and *in-spired* (bringing the breath of God and spirit into form). Each of these play-on-words elucidate that when consciousness shifts, time and space drop away, and change can be immediately *in-bodied* (embodied). We need immediate intimacy, or *in-to-me-see*, so that there is clarity and transparency in our illumination and we can create instant karma; that is, alter a karmic relationship in a moment. Because in the shamanic world there is the possibility of space-time hopping, a portal can be created through shape-shifting our conscious awareness that allows us to see the whole story played out from beginning to end. I call this seeing the "bigger picture" instead of only a small fragment of reality. The instant we see the big story versus our ego's limited story and perspective, our reality is automatically changed within our own psyche. Once this occurs everything about the situation energetically begins to change. As we transform our consciousness, bringing in this future self and future world through the imagination first, we create a quickening within our being, as with imminent birth when a woman's body knows that the ring of fire is open and birth is happening whether she is ready or not. By definition, it is the right, or ripe, time for birth because the opening exists and nothing can stop it from happening. When we view the world from a place of love and trust, everything becomes possible—and it becomes possible right now. We personify that love, thus granting the spirit the power to accelerate consciousness and action, first in the inner world and then in the outer world. By creating opportunity for the *in-sights* (inner sight) needed to bring forth the *in-formation* (insight brought into form) for transformation, the outer world can change *in-stantly*.

In life we all face significant outer-world experiences, such as the death of a loved one or loss of a job, or collective experiences like natural disasters, global warming, pandemics, and the varied reactions to all of these that cause devastation to our outer world. These experiences create a radical shift and change within, because they alter our state of consciousness. They shock and dissociate us from normal reality so something else can break through. But this type of change still comes from a place of woe. When we consciously choose to undergo a radical shift in our perspective by engaging in purposeful altered states of consciousness, as we do with shamanic initiations, we are able to use imagination to awaken our inner selves, doing so from a place of wisdom instead of woe. Either way, it is time to wake up!

One of my dearest and earliest brilliant mystical transpersonal teachers, Jacquelyn Small—founder of the Eupsychia Institute, which focused on Integrative Breathwork—frequently used to say, "True mystery teachings can't be taught, but they can be caught." To "catch" them, however, we must be willing to forget everything we think we know and open ourselves to the Great Mystery. Jacquelyn believed deeply that everyone had an inner healer, no matter how lost or confused their human self had become, and that each of us just needed to find a way to wake up and remember our true self. Upon the awakening of this internal sleeping giant, all wisdom is available to all of us, not just to an elite individual or special group. It was through Jacquelyn's profound mystery school teachings, which included learning how to journey inward with special breathing methods, symbolism, and group sharing that I was deeply touched in those early years of my searching. My faith in myself grew roots, and I discovered deep wisdom that had been buried beneath society's repressive rules and expectations.

The inner tools of shamanism provide a map for seeking and living from a place of shamanic consciousness. To begin our discussion of these methods, I will first explore the process of learning to shape-shift into and through the energetic fields of past, present, and future. To awaken the Aquarian Shaman within is to take the journey back in time to untangle energetic patterns that affect our current reality, then reclaim aspects of ourselves that were lost in childhood or even in a past life, and in so doing, recognize our own power and energize ourselves to live our current lives from a place of wholeness. When we have accessed and brought healing to pieces of the past, we begin living more fully in the present moment, and in alignment with our core values and authentic natures. From this place of alignment and personal freedom and responsibility, we can then shape-shift into our future selves and download those future selves into present time. In this way, learning to walk the spiral path of transformation becomes an accelerated process for consciously and wisely embodying the change we wish to see in the world, and more readily showing up for our deeper purpose. If every person on the planet underwent this accelerated process and lived every day from this state of awakened perspective, rather than living through shadow projections and personal wounding, the world would become that change we wish to see. However, we cannot ask the world to magically change; the deep inner work of soulful transformation must start from within human beings, one moment at a time, and radiate outward to heal and bless all our relations.

As I began to remember my true self in my late twenties and early thirties, my life force energy woke up and became unstoppable. Prior to this awakening, I had fallen into addictions and self-defeating unconscious behaviors that created major roadblocks, keeping me stuck in low self-esteem and soul loss. I knew that something was wrong and that I felt stuck, but I was living in a dazed state, unable to access my human will to make lasting changes to old toxic patterns.

One evening I literally cried out loud for help to the universe, pleading for whatever was out there and loved me to take my life and will into its care and to show me what to do. Shortly after this, my whole world began to shift and the road before me opened. I still had to put forth the effort to take each step on that road, but I was aware that some unseen, benevolent force was traveling close by my side. I was no longer muddling through on my own, with my ego demanding that life be on its terms; instead I had entered into uncharted territory, and even though it was scary, it somehow seemed familiar, as if I had come home to a place I knew long ago. I have since had the joy and privilege of sharing this journey of discovery with countless others. It is my sincere hope and prayer that the tools and techniques offered here will help ignite the fires of your own inner shaman. May your soul's longing open the door to a heartfelt passion for life and freedom, as mine once did.

I remember, early on my path, listening over and over to a song called "Return Again," which spoke to how I felt inside. Below are some of the lyrics to that song. To "return" is something we do over and over as an awakened shaman, and one can feel the spiral path emerge in these simple song lyrics. I invite you to see if they awaken something in you too:

> *Return again . . .*
> *Return to the land of your soul . . .*
> *Return to where you are*
> *Born and reborn again . . .*

On the spiral path of transformation, we encounter fairly predictable cycles of change as we journey to return to ourselves. The SHIP method, which I created to support this transformation, invites us to consciously engage each life phase of dissolution and reconstruction.

Once we understand how each of the cycles of change—water, earth, fire, spirit, and air—are associated with characteristic experiences and feelings, we can learn to quickly identify what cycle we are in. Having done so, we'll know what kind of support we need and how to optimize our growth through that cycle, thus ensuring we don't get stuck there indefinitely.

12

SHIP to Transport You Back to Yourself

SHIP is the Shamanic Healing Initiatory Process—an "inner tools" map I created to support others in navigating the spiral path of transformation. The program, established in the year 2000, caters to those seeking structured shamanic training. It offers a clear process with milestones for personal healing and awakening, providing a framework for individuals to deconstruct, reconstruct, and re-member their inner selves. The most important fundamental principle of SHIP is to provide people with a map for the nature of how human beings change. I found over my many years of working as a therapist that people who were not living their purpose and thriving generally fell into two categories. They either got "stuck in the muck," becoming overly identified with their wounding so they could not climb out, or they were in spiritual bypass, dissociated from their bodies and wounding experiences. In both cases, these people were disconnected from their hearts and were not fully embodied in their lives.

To step onto the spiral path is to investigate who we are. In this investigation, we must look first to what came before on our journey; in other words, we must look back to our childhood to understand the roots of present-day habits that may not be serving us. We should first consider our family of origin, whose characteristics and trials may still be affecting our current psyche. The purpose of this inventory of our childhood is not to blame our parents or guardians for who we are, but rather to understand that much of what we do is in reaction to unconsciously held beliefs or coping skills created in response to childhood relationships and experiences. As much as we may think we are aware of our wounds, there are always parts that remain hidden from us. An honest inventory of our childhood and upbringing allows us to see how it may have contributed to who we are today and the circumstances we have created in our lives. While a deep exploration is necessary, it is also important not to overly identify with the wounds we uncover and thus fall into the trap of defining ourselves by them. In a healthy, honest inventory, we should be able to fully experience our past struggles and the feelings they provoke, so they can move through us and not get lodged in the unconscious long term.

Every one of us is connected to the cosmic tree of life, and although we come through our parents, we belong to ourselves and to a bigger picture. As we acknowledge and honor the wounds and the gifts from our lineage and ancestors, we recognize that there is an ancestral or family tree within the cosmic tree. If you have a spouse or partner, maybe they sometimes accuse you of being like your mother or father. Or, on the flip side, you may be proud of certain traits passed on to you by a family member. We cannot help but carry within us aspects of our family tree, but when you look at this reality with a fresh perspective, you may pinpoint inherited traits and habits that unconsciously cause you suffering. Reclaiming your original true self from these overlays of learned behavior liberates your creativity and energy. It is up to us all to fly free from our parents and culture and to be true to our authentic selves, while still recognizing and honoring the lessons of our shadow wounding.

The process of SHIP creates an inner pathway to awaken our Aquarian Shaman. This wise one inside us offers insight, opportunity, and support for a high level of reflection and subsequent right action in our lives. The spiral path also reminds us that these wounds, behaviors, or traits we uncover are not a one-time deal. We will revisit these places over time and through our evolution because they are the core teachers for our soul's development. It is important to remember this as our journey unfolds, so that we don't get caught up in thinking we've failed because an old wound or habit resurfaces during a time of stress, change, or upheaval. It re-emerges so we can enter the next stage of our evolution with this wounding information in hand. When we have the spiral path to use as a map, we can engage our inner GPS or compass, adjust course, and find compassion and forgiveness for ourselves and others on the imperfectly perfect human journey.

Each SHIP initiation consists of creating sacred space for the Shamanic Breathwork journeying process described in more detail in Chapter 17. These shamanic initiations support each participant in awakening and connecting with their inner shaman. You can keep these teachings and initiations in mind even when you journey, meditate, or do Shamanic Breathwork at home alone. When we hold an intention to uncover and discover these hidden shamanic aspects of ourselves, we will more readily open to and receive what is needed for our growth.

SHIP is a series of six highly transformative initiations designed to accelerate and awaken shamanic consciousness. The purpose of these initiations is to assist individuals and professionals in learning how to embody shamanic consciousness by journeying beyond the limitations of their ego identity, and shape-shifting into their soul's sacred purpose. The personal evolutionary growth experienced through these shamanic initiations lets individuals embrace shamanic tools to create real and lasting change in their lives. They are able to transform previous struggles that continue to impact them, and thus reclaim personal passion and power by remembering who they truly are. A deepening connection to unconditional love for self and others can occur, enhancing the shaman's ability to support others through volatile times by sharing their unique gifts and sacred purpose with the world.

13
Working with Archetypes on the Spiral Path

Before we begin describing in detail the six SHIP initiations that make up the map of the spiral path of transformation, I want to expound on the language of archetypes, which informs and guides us along the path. I mentioned earlier how archetypes relate to the act of playing with identity and expression, and how, through that play, we develop our "good medicine" chest. Archetypes provide templates for the imagination, enabling us to envision experiences beyond our current self-understanding. They offer insights into various identities, such as a police officer, doctor, healer, child, parent, lover, or royalty, and even divine figures like gods or goddesses. Archetypes also provide models to explain the behavior of nature elements, animals, and even the weather. We might say something like, "Gosh, I felt swept up in a storm," or, "I felt like a cornered animal." In these instances, one articulates the experience of embodying an archetype, where our imagination translates the essence of that archetype into tangible feelings, thoughts, and emotions.

Just as children immerse themselves in play, embodying roles like "rocket scientist," adults can tap into subconscious archetypes to transform or cultivate new facets of their being. By focusing on the essence of these archetypes, we can "wear" their attributes for a time, aiding ourselves in healing or in taking up new, embodied roles.

For instance, if we aspire to be a writer but are uncertain where to start, we might invoke the archetype of a revered novelist or poet, alive or dead. We can then harmonize with the essence of that individual's craft, experiencing and emulating what it feels like to connect with their literary prowess. We might even look to a god who mythologically takes the form of an archetypal scribe, such as the god Thoth in Egypt or Cadmus in Greece. We might study these gods, their history and mythology, to better understand the challenges and joys of being a writer, and what practices they employ; we might even dress like them to further playact our possible future writer self.

As a second example, to transform a limiting belief such as "I don't feel worthy," we might engage with various archetypes. We might first get in touch with the "peasant" or "bag lady" archetype as an image of an unconscious feeling we have about ourselves. These archetypes help us see how we feel "less than" or "impoverished" in some way. This in turn may help explain a self-defeating behavior that we have allowed to operate in our lives. Once this particular archetype has brought to us its vital message and healing, we might be introduced in our psyche to another archetype, like the "king" or "queen," reflecting another aspect of ourselves that has been tucked away. Once we have seen and moved through one aspect of belief or wounding, like "I am not worthy," and reclaimed lost parts of ourselves associated with that belief, then we can move into an empowered vision of our future self, symbolically represented by the king or queen. In this example, we may not be accustomed to feeling the power of personal sovereignty and agency, so by turning our attention toward the archetypes of king and queen, we can don the royal robe, so to speak, and practice every day what it is to be sovereign in our own lives, until one day we find that we are naturally inhabiting that form. The more of ourselves, the light and the dark, that we claim from our unconscious, the more whole we become. This process of reclamation is truly the essence of what it takes to awaken the inner healer and embody the Aquarian Shaman in the outer world.

As we grow in self-acceptance, we begin to discern the richness of our being and the boundless potential for what we can achieve. This understanding reveals our "awakening" to be an ongoing odyssey—delving into profound depths and ascending to new pinnacles of possibility that reside within each person and across humanity. It is a journey of magical and mystical layers, involving multiple dimensions, and its potential is endless when we move willingly toward a higher sphere of being and work with the wisdom of the archetypes, especially the Aquarian energies of higher love and wisdom that strive through our thoughts and energy fields to create monumental changes in, through, and around us in the world.

As children, instinctively tapping into archetypes is second nature when exploring our aspirations. In adulthood, we often cloak this simple, innate curiosity with complex language and methodologies, always seeking a rational explanation. But as we transcend adult-imposed fears and judgments, we find the freedom to embrace our true selves, engaging in life's magic and playfulness and co-creating our dream existence with ease.

With the above examples as a reference point, we can now address some of the "adult" terminology regarding archetypes. Joseph Campbell, the twentieth century's foremost expert on world mythology, explained that archetypes—elements of the collective unconscious that elude direct observation—are most accessibly interpreted through the lens of myth. As he wrote in his book *The Hero with a Thousand Faces*, "The symbols of mythology are not manufactured; they cannot be ordered, invented, or permanently suppressed. They are spontaneous productions of the psyche." According to academyofideas.com, "As manifestations of the deepest layers of the unconscious, myths are thought to reveal timeless truths about the yearnings, fears, and aspirations common to every individual." Carl Jung said, "Myths are first and foremost psychic phenomena that reveal the nature of the soul."

The "Hero's Journey" that Joseph Campbell described mirrors the psychological growth of the individual. This path to authenticity necessitates the process of individuation, wherein one's true self is reflected through relationships with others and is explored through the unconscious. Integration of this hidden realm with our conscious self reveals our true personality. We can unearth these depths by interpreting dreams or engaging with myths, often unknowingly experienced through the narratives of Hollywood films. In his book *Pathways to Bliss*, Joseph Campbell states, "These [mythological] symbols stem from the psyche; they speak from and to the spirit. And they are in fact the vehicles of communication between the deeper depths of our spiritual life and this relatively thin layer of consciousness by which we govern our daylight existences."

The unconscious holds untapped potential that, when realized and merged with our conscious awareness, catalyzes personal growth. These principles form the SHIP process's foundation, aiming to awaken the Aquarian Shaman within by unlocking these latent capabilities—our future self. By embarking on SHIP's initiatory path, we engage in our own Hero's or Heroine's Journey, guided by archetypes through the unconscious netherworld. We seek to recover and illuminate our hidden places, thus actualizing the innate potential encoded in our DNA and the energy that surrounds us all.

The Sumerian myth "The Descent of Inanna" (ca. 1900–1600 BCE) serves as a classic example of the Hero's Journey. It recounts Inanna's descent from heaven to the underworld to meet her sister Ereshkigal, Queen of the Dead. Inanna must make a sacrifice before she can leave the world of the dead and return to the world above. The poem begins, "From the Great Above she opened her ear to the Great Below," signifying Inanna's call to a journey she doesn't yet comprehend. This story reveals that venturing into the underworld demands leaving behind all that is familiar, without the comfort of a guaranteed return. It's a journey of faith, surrender, and trust, on which the heroine learns through truths revealed, and then emerges transformed, integrating new wisdom into her very essence.

On the shamanic spiral path, we encounter teachers who carry "archetypal messages" for our psyches. "Archetypal" by definition means to be typical of a particular person, place, or thing. The term is most often used to indicate repeating symbols, themes, or motifs in literature, poetry, art, and especially mythology. An archetype is a prototype or a blueprint from which similar entities are derived. Carl Jung's work describes archetypes as emanations of the collective unconscious, surfacing in dreams, myths, stories, and altered-state journeys. They are the soul's language, and our imagination is key to interpreting these symbols in order to aid our personal growth.

When we contemplate archetypes as larger patterns in nature, mythology, psychology, and theology that help us acknowledge and describe our own humanity, we become aware of a natural pattern and rhythm to our own personal journey. Thus we can find meaning and purpose in life's events as archetypal initiations encountered by every person, which help make up the larger story of existence. By adopting a bird's-eye-view perspective, we can appreciate the wisdom woven into the fabric of our individual experiences.

Along the spiral path, we work with the elements of water, earth, fire, spirit, and air in an archetypal way. Each element carries natural rhythms, colors, textures, characteristics, and behaviors that help us understand our "Hero's Journey," and which we can look to as an outside reference point to give meaning to that which transpires within ourselves. Animal totems, gods, goddesses, mythological creatures, fairy-tale characters, and theological prophets all work with our psyches in this way, by providing metaphor, patterns, and symbols to us for our own interpretation, based on what we need to learn and bring forth from our unconscious world. Archetypes are universal cosmic patterns presented to us through our imagination and human senses.

Embracing the shamanic path means engaging with the elements and archetypes that guide our transformative journeys. Our imagination allows us to suspend linear thinking and connect with our inner selves. This approach encourages a return to the open, curious mind of childhood, tapping into various archetypes to unlock personal growth. Ultimately, it invites us to play with the archetype of the shaman, the one who can shape-shift and perpetually try on new ways of being, enhancing our innate human potential.

14
The SHIP Cycles of Change
Water, Earth, Fire, Spirit, and Air

The shamanic path teaches us to recognize life as a journey, acknowledging our past, present, future, and the voice of our inner guide, and to honor these facets of ourselves again and again through a lifetime of cyclical change. In contrast to the uninitiated view that seeks a final "happily ever after" or feels defeated by change, shamanic practice embraces continual learning through change and transformation. It's an acceptance of life's cycles, allowing us to experience a consciousness that evolves through perpetual symbolic death and rebirth, without true endings or beginnings, only a spectrum of energetic experiences.

Long before we physically die, every cell in our bodies will continually die and be renewed or re-created. This is how the body's immune system gets rid of cells that have done their job but are now ragged and weary and need to be replaced, so we can continue to function optimally. Over a period of seven years, we will re-create and regenerate every cell in our bodies—in other words, you are literally a whole new person every seven years! Our physical bodies and our emotional bodies go through symbolic death and rebirth throughout our time on this planet. No matter how hard we might try, we are not going to remain the same people in body or spirit throughout the whole of our lives. We will go through change, whether consciously or not. Life is an evolving dance, not a straight path toward some final imagined victory. By actively engaging with life's rhythms, we intentionally grow and embrace change. We celebrate triumphs, learn from losses, and dive into creativity, finding purpose in nature's cycles. This mindful approach infuses meaning into every moment, liberates us from fear, and deepens our spiritual journey. Without it, we risk stagnation and unfulfilled potential.

The spiral path can be exhilarating, playful, magical, and miraculous. It can also be messy, scary, and lonely for a time while we recalibrate. However when we push through to the other side of the transformation, we find that new people meet us on the path, and new creations come into our lives. The temptation at this point is to say, "Ta-da! I've made it!" Yes, you have made it, and it's important to celebrate your effort and allow yourself nourishing time to rest—you worked hard to get here! It is also wonderful to allow others to celebrate your accomplishment, perhaps with a special ceremony. They will feel good about giving to you in this way—even if you're someone who's not entirely comfortable having your achievements recognized. Nonetheless, the biggest stumbling block to change is the expectation that you will maintain a steady state of "having made it," and the accompanying feeling of failure when the "ta-da!" moment inevitably and necessarily doesn't last forever. Honoring life's peaks without clinging to them is crucial for emotional well-being. We must accept the impermanence of all phases, joyful or challenging, so as to continue in our growth.

The spiral path of transformation takes us on a cycle through the elements—water, earth, fire, spirit, and air. With practice we can move through the cycles more quickly, but early on, it is not uncommon to find ourselves "stuck" in one of the elements. There are both lighter and denser energetic components to each element—some might view these as positive and negative aspects, but that perspective can lead to judgment of our experiences. The lighter energy of an element is the part that emerges when we are in a healthy balance with that element. The denser energy arises when we feel stuck or are unable to move through that element. In confronting these denser energies, we will be well-served by seeking support from others who can help shepherd us through the depths; after all, we are not meant to navigate life's challenges alone.

Every individual has a unique relationship with these elements, and some elements may feel more comfortable to you than others, depending on your personal makeup and life experiences. However, as we learn to appreciate what each element brings to our attention and our lives, we're better able to move with each element in a healthy dance, wherein we can engage with each element for just the right amount of time needed for growth, evolution, and wholeness.

So, let us now explore what these cycles of change look like in practice. We can begin anywhere on the spiral path, and we often find ourselves in different elemental cycles relative to different facets of our lives. As an example, we may feel that we are in a place of fire and action in our work world, but are experiencing our primary love relationship to be in a watery renewal cycle. It is also possible that one can move through multiple cycles in the course of a day. Thus, the elemental spiral path template can help us to know where we are starting on the path in any given moment. That said, for the purpose of describing the cycles of elemental transformation, the natural place to begin is with the element of water.

FIRST CYCLE OF CHANGE

Water: The Sacred Wheel of Life and the Spiral Path

You would measure time the measureless and the immeasurable . . .
And that which sings and contemplates in you is still dwelling within the bounds of that first moment which scattered the stars into space . . .
But if in your thought you must measure time into

seasons, let each season encircle all the other seasons,
And let today embrace the past with remembrance
and the future with longing.

"On Time," from
The Prophet by Kahlil Gibran

Water is the element of our life's beginning, the place where our cellular DNA messages create the form of our body while gestating in the waters of the womb. This element is crucial to our survival, as over seventy percent of the human body is composed of water. Every cell in our bodies is bathed in an aqueous environment and requires water to transmit messages from one cell to another. In the same way, we require an outer relationship with the water element to receive the cosmic messages contained both within our DNA and in the Great Mystery. Our cellular DNA is just a hologram for the universal DNA—or structural nature of the universe—and it is through the physical as well as the archetypal medium of water that the universal messages are transmitted to our own cellular DNA.

The first SHIP initiation onto the spiral path, then, is a dive into the archetypal water cycle. Utilizing meditation or the Shamanic Breathwork journey process, we may re-enter our original womb experience and our birth process. This may lead to a sensation of being in a space of pure nothingness or openness, which I often refer to as "the void." To enter the void is to step into a plane of existence where time, space, and physical form do not exist. It is in this void that we can retrieve crucial energetic information that may not yet have been processed through the mind, body, or imagination. The void is a place of universal record-keeping for the soul. When we enter the void, we often receive important downloads from the soul and from our original source, the Great Mystery.

Entering this water cycle can allow us to experience deep rest, contentment, and peace. In our contemporary culture where workaholism is encouraged, many people are lacking time, space, or motivation to enter into this very necessary state of replenishment. When a person is unwilling or unable to enter the water cycle and thus to temper the fiery nature of workaholism, it can cause burnout, and might lead to the habitual use of substances, sex, or food to find a release from the tension.

The water cycle can also manifest as a denser energetic experience, in which there is a longing to return to an imagined place of safety and nurturance. This longing can lead to serial comfort-seeking through addictions, or can cause a person to get stuck in apathy, hopelessness, or obsessive-compulsive planning without action. When someone is stuck in the water cycle, they may have wonderful ideas but are unable to take the necessary action to bring their dreams to reality. For those who had negative womb experiences, it may feel unsafe to enter the birth canal and birth oneself and one's ideas into the world. This can lead to inability and helplessness when it comes to manifesting one's goals. An individual in this situation might need support to get through the birth canal and take action. In other words, an especially "watery" person might consider how to cultivate more of the fire element within.

SECOND CYCLE OF CHANGE

Earth: Honoring the Ancestors and Re-membering the Cosmic Tree of Life

Your children are not your children.
They are the sons and daughters of Life's longing for itself.
They come through you but not from you,
And though they are with you yet they belong not to you.
You may give them your love but not your thoughts,
For they have their own thoughts.

You may house their bodies but not their souls,
For their souls dwell in the house of tomorrow, which you
cannot visit, not even in your dreams.

"On Children," from
The Prophet by Kahlil Gibran

After being in the waters and awakening to our original womb experiences, the next natural place to find ourselves on the spiral path is entering the birth canal, where we encounter our family-of-origin patterns. This is the archetypal earth cycle. It is very common as we enter the restrictive space of the metaphorical birth canal to feel some discomfort, confusion, and a sense of helplessness. We cannot go back to the womb, but the ring of fire of imminent birth has not yet opened. When we reach this place on the spiral path, we often confront feelings of limitation and boundary issues. On the lighter side of this earth element, when we are able to find clarity regarding our process, this cycle offers an opportunity to willingly embrace the need to be grounded in body and in life. We can then begin to explore real-world options and break through dreamy illusions to take practical action. From this place, we are able to slow down and make grounded decisions for next steps. We find relief by taking action that needs to be taken in order to prepare for the healthy birth of a new idea or way of being.

At this point on the spiral path, we should practice healthy ego engagement, take care of the mundane details of life, balance reasoning with creativity and humility, break out of denial and be honest with ourselves and others, and recognize what is not working in our lives. This methodical inventory allows us to take care of our physical needs, develop strong boundaries to be able to parent ourselves, and take care of our feelings and our energy in order to enter the next stage of the spiral path—the alchemical fires of transformation.

THIRD CYCLE OF CHANGE

Fire: Soul Loss and Reclaiming the Shadow

Your joy is your sorrow unmasked.
And the selfsame well from which your laughter rises was
oftentimes filled with your tears.
And how else can it be?
The deeper that sorrow carves into your being, the more joy
you can contain.
. . . When you are joyous, look deep into your heart and you
shall find it is only that which has given you sorrow that is
giving you joy.

"ON JOY AND SORROW," FROM
THE PROPHET BY KAHLIL GIBRAN

As we enter the third cycle of transformation, the element of fire, we come to the archetypal cervix of birth, also known as the ring of fire. At this place along the path, birth is imminent; there is no turning back without losing ground, and there is no staying where we are. The only way out is to go through. The energy of this element, fire, is filled with a sense of urgency, a need to take action. It presents a feeling of "now or never." Feelings of anxiety, impatience, or irritability may be provoked when we feel a need for change. These symptoms can lead us to seek out a way to alleviate our discomfort, and it is important at this point to find a healthy way to express the tension created by fire. When we can acknowledge and release these feelings in a safe space, there is a free-ing up of creative potential energy that can be used in a proactive and productive way. This movement into creative action catalyzes us to give birth to our new selves.

Many people are uncomfortable with or even afraid of this power-ful energy within, especially if it surfaces as anger. When this energy is disowned because of our fear of it, we can regress back into the earth cycle, seeking a sense of safety and thus getting stuck and losing the forward momentum of the cyclical process. When we backslide in this way, it may take a great deal of time, energy, and effort to regain our footing on the path.

In the same way that fire in nature can be erratic and devastating when out of control, this third cycle in a person's life can become chaotic, full of turmoil and confusion. In other words, change can be messy. We may have less grace than we would like in letting go of patterns, relationships, or jobs that no longer are in our best interest, in order to make room for the new. However as we navigate change, it is important to keep in our mind and heart that we don't always need to burn the entire house down in order to do some inner remodeling. When we can find grace and patience to know that with time, out of the chaos, a new form will take shape, we'll be better able to navigate the challenges that come with the upheaval. By the same token, in our impatience for something to change, but without the infrastructure in place to guide us wisely through, we may end up continually tearing down our houses and never rebuilding from within. This leaves us feeling barren and empty, with no sense of purpose or direction.

During this cycle, acknowledging our past actions and future course, coupled with grace and mindful surrender, can guide us through the transition. We're invited to embrace a leap of faith in which we dare to act expansively without certainty of the results. As we gain experience on the path, our self-trust deepens, enhancing our co-creative evolution and our ability to make these leaps with confidence and conviction. We learn to believe in the wisdom of the process, rather than allowing anxiety and fear to hold us back.

This third cycle allows us to confront and reclaim a part of our consciousness called "the shadow"—in other words, aspects of ourselves that have been hidden away and may be unconsciously sabotaging our growth. When we step into the fires of transformation, the pieces of ourselves that come forward to be reclaimed may feel uncomfortable to us and to those who share our lives. Yet reclaiming those parts of ourselves is ultimately vital to our well-being and, in the end, can be positive in nature.

FOURTH CYCLE OF CHANGE

Spirit: Opening to the Beloved: Contacting your Spiritual Helpers and Guides

Your soul is oftentimes a battlefield, upon which
your reason and your judgment wage war against
your passion and your appetite.
Would that I could be the peacemaker in your
soul, that I might turn the discord and the rivalry of
your elements into oneness and melody.
But how shall I, unless you yourselves be also the
peacemakers, nay, the lovers of all your elements?

"ON REASON AND PASSION," FROM
THE PROPHET BY KAHLIL GIBRAN

The fourth cycle on the spiral path is the transpersonal element of Spirit, of super-nature, or the supernatural. Up to this point on the path the cycles have been of a personal nature, referring us back to our human self. In the cycle of spirit, we go beyond the personal to that which infuses our human form with energy and vitality. It is in this cycle that we release everything of the human struggle, and surrender to love. This is where we find grace and divine support from supernatural beings and spiritual allies. Here we find a calm, peaceful faith that we will be helped in making changes as we manifest our new octave of being, in the co-creative alliance between the human vessel and the spirit that infuses our vessel. In this cycle, we turn everything over to our own higher authority and release the ego's agenda and need for control. When we have done our part and laid the foundation for our next evolution, it is no longer up to us alone to make it happen, and we know we'll have support from other realms when it comes time to implement the necessary changes.

It is in the cycle of spirit that we willingly place everything we think we know, and everything we possess, upon the sacrificial altar, trusting that what is meant to remain ours will remain, and what no longer serves us will be taken in its current form and renewed, recycled, or regenerated in some way that is for the highest good of all. This is the arena of high alchemy, where magic, mystery, and synchronicity come into the mix of our transformation, transmutation, and possibly transfiguration.

As with all the cycles, if we lose consciousness during this spirit cycle, we can fall into the shadow side of this element and become complacent. Complacency can lead to giving up or giving in and taking no personal responsibility in the transformation process. Remember that "surrender" is a verb, a dynamic action word. When we step to the edge of the chasm between what is and what will be, the fires of change push us forward into the abyss and into a conscious free fall. We are not falling as a rag doll; we are actively diving and trusting with eyes wide open, embracing a new way of being human. This is the moment when we come to know and feel seen by the "inner beloved," the sacred other, which is in fact a part of ourselves returning home to aid us. What once seemed out of reach now fills us with a sense of divine union and wholeness. This shift launches us into the next cycle: that of air, rebirth, integration, and celebration.

FIFTH CYCLE OF CHANGE

Air: Awakening to the Aquarian Shaman Within

You give but little when you give of your
possessions.
It is when you give of yourself that you truly give.

"ON GIVING," FROM
THE PROPHET BY KAHLIL GIBRAN

The fifth cycle, the element of air, is the archetypal experience of rebirth. This is a time of celebration and of taking a deep, spacious breath as we integrate and find meaning and understanding in all that has transpired during the previous four cycles. From the air element, we are able to fly above our human journey and see the big picture, gleaning its wisdom that we can then share, whether as a teacher, counselor, guide, writer, or leader. We feel a sense of freedom and openness. All our energetic centers, or chakras, are open and able to receive the deep breath of our being, all the way into the lower, human chakras. As the upper chakras and lower chakras come into union within the heart center, a new alignment arises. In other words, all our energy is given to our soul's sacred purpose. From this place of rebirth within the air element, we are propelled toward sacred service to the planet and humanity.

This cycle is associated with considerable relief and joy, along with a sense of completion. Yet we may need to take a few turns on the spiral path before we understand that this feeling of "having arrived," while worthy of celebration, can set us up for disappointment when we find that to continue evolving as a soul, we will need to journey onward from this place. When we can maintain the newfound wisdom from the air cycle, and also retain the humility and "beginner's mind" of the initiate, our decisions and choices will be in accord with the multidimensional truth of our being rather than oriented toward linear conquest.

Understanding "arrival" as a transient stop on the spiral path can prevent feelings of failure in not maintaining "expert" status. By embracing growth over perfection, a teacher retains a student's mindset, inviting freedom and playfulness into their endeavors. This mindset shift—away from relentless perfectionism toward compassion and humor—allows us to see from the high vantage point of the air cycle that there is yet another level on the spiral path. Through this sixth, final cycle, we can bring our imagination to a larger field of energy and invoke the next version of our future self.

SIXTH CYCLE OF CHANGE

Activating your Future Self

Say not, "I have found the truth," but rather, "I have found a truth."
Say not, "I have found the path of the soul." Say rather, "I have met the soul walking upon my path."
For the soul walks upon all paths.
The soul walks not upon a line, neither does it grow like a reed.
The soul unfolds itself, like a lotus of countless petals.

"ON SELF-KNOWLEDGE," FROM
THE PROPHET BY KAHLIL GIBRAN

When we invoke this future self, we will be engaging with an aspect of ourselves that is first imagined, and then is ours to make manifest. This future self will need to be cultivated, and we will need to grow into it. To take on the growth required to manifest this future self, we must willingly begin once again on the spiral path—live, die, transform, rest, reinvent, grow, repeat!

Each of us is an avatar with the ability to humbly and confidently bring our divine god-self into physical form in our daily lives. "Avatar," by the Merriam-Webster definition, is "an embodiment (as of a concept or philosophy) often in a person." The definition goes on to indicate that:

Avatar derives from a Sanskrit word meaning "descent," and when it first appeared in English in the late 18th century, it referred to the descent of a deity to the earth—typically, the incarnation in earthly form of Vishnu or another Hindu deity. It later came to refer to any incarnation in human form, and then to any embodiment (such as that of a concept or philosophy), whether or not in the form of a person. In the age of technology, *avatar* has developed another sense—it can now be used for the image that a person chooses as his or her "embodiment" in an electronic medium.

For me, this embodiment of our future self—be it described as an avatar, shaman, or superhero—is the involution required to accelerate evolution. There are several definitions of involution. As it is best defined for our purposes, involution is "a process that occurs when something turns in upon itself," "the act or an instance of enfolding," or "an inward curvature or penetration." In other words, we allow our future self to penetrate our current form, to enfold that future self into being in the current self. This is what it is to bring multidimensional consciousness to humanity through each of our individual human vessels. More and more of us are becoming walkers between worlds, as evidenced by the increasing number of books and other media discussing multidimensional being and perception.

One way I like to further explore this multidimensionality is through the concept of the avatar or the superhero, both of which are ubiquitous in our popular culture today. Why is our culture attracted to superheroes and villains? Is there something hidden in the shadows, a subliminal part of us that they represent or tap into? Do we ourselves have the potential to awaken these abilities of heightened sensitivity, so as to sense changes in our environment, pick up warning signals, appreciate the symbolism of a message from nature, and ultimately to use this information to do good? The answer, in my experience, is yes. We can become the superheroes of our own lives. We are the avatars who can align with our higher, noble, god-selves and embody sacred purpose and planetary service. Something in our consciousness has been looking outward for the superhero, the one who will save us from current circumstances, but we need to shift consciousness and recognize that the one who will save us is us. The shaman, avatar, or superhero lies within. I encourage you to be a superhero in your life—see things, hear things, sense things, and use your power for good.

In childhood and beyond, our fascination with villains and superheroes speaks to our innate sense of dormant flaws and potential strengths. These larger-than-life figures resonate with us, reflecting unawakened aspects of our being. The rise in superhero films isn't mere coincidence but synchronicity—archetypes reaching us through art, media, and culture, shaping our beliefs. They become a kind of family to us, touching our hearts and awakening future selves poised to contribute positively to the world. Engaging with these archetypes doesn't just use our physical senses but connects with our higher consciousness, our inner avatar.

As a modern-day reference for the avatar concept, the 2009 movie *Avatar* depicted an everyman protagonist who employs futuristic technology to send his consciousness into an altered version of himself. This new self, or avatar, has experiences of connecting with Indigenous wisdom and magical, mystical communion with animals, trees, and the natural environment. The protagonist is introduced to a way of being that is interconnected with the web of life. In his other, supposedly more "human" reality, he is at first aligned with, but then ends up fighting against, the patriarchal system that seeks to mine the magical Indigenous environment for its natural resources. As the movie progresses, the patriarchy attempts to destroy the mystical land; however, the huge sacred tree, which the Indigenous people live within and depend upon, maintains its strong roots and vitality deep underground despite everything on the surface being burned down and blown up. This is a wonderful metaphor for our lives—when we can grow our inner roots deeply, no amount of turmoil on the surface can destroy us, as our vitality will rise up anew from the rubble, like a phoenix from the ashes.

As our main character progresses along his heroic journey, we witness his personal battle to understand right and wrong, where his loyalties lie, and how he identifies his core values, in his struggle to decide between a life of connection to the Indigenous community and magical land, or the base human desires driven by greed. In the end he chooses the life of his avatar body, his higher-octave future self, a choice so complete that he no longer needs the assistance of a machine portal, or altered state, to access that life. He finally emerges into oneness with the avatar, his divine essence, and it becomes his new way of being.

Like the protagonist in *Avatar* who evolves into a connected, empowered leader, we too must nurture our potential selves daily. This evolution requires embracing new skills and perspectives, staying humble, and being open to starting anew. Wisdom from past experiences informs us, yet we must not hold onto it rigidly; instead, we must allow growth and shed that which no longer serves us. As we evolve, we make space for grander dreams, moving beyond the notion that value comes from holding a fixed status in the world. Stagnation is the enemy of our nature, which thrives on change and creativity. Dreams fuel our soul and our collective progress; nurturing them against doubt and negativity is vital. Your dreams are your own, deserving of protection and encouragement.

I urge you to become whatever new avatar is speaking to you. Do so over and over again by tending to your dreams and practicing every day the new skills and perceptions needed to fulfill and embody that vision. On the journey to becoming your future self, practice self-compassion for the part of you that feels vulnerable when learning new skills; remember, initial awkwardness is part of the growth process. Look upon this new and developing you with the same kindness and love you would show a toddler learning to walk. Don't expect instant mastery; humility and a sense of humor are of great value at this learning stage. When we put aside our egocentric wish for perfection, we are better able to ask for help and support from those who might aid us—whether they be gods or goddesses, nature beings, archetypal and ancestral guides, or compassionate human allies who may already have achieved dreams similar to ours. Embracing new skills with joy and a focus on dreams over perfectionism allows us to approach personal growth with light-heartedness, even as we seriously pursue our aspirations. This balance embodies the playful yet purposeful progression toward our envisioned future and greater contributions to the world.

15

Embodying the Five Elemental Cycles

Having now described the fundamental principles and characteristics of each cycle of change, and the archetypal elements of each cycle, let's explore how we might begin to play with these elements, and exercise new inner-world muscles to develop a regular practice of moving through transformation in a creative, shape-shifting way. Depending on your personal experience of each element, you may wish to create a deeper connection with some of them, while also attending to elements that are especially strong in your being so they don't get out of balance. In the following exercises, I will provide a framework for the possible ways to enter into and engage with the elements and cycles in your own life and your own home.

First, we create an elemental space. Whenever I engage in communion with another entity, be it a nature element, animal, spirit guide, or another human, I create a sacred space. This goes back to some of our discussions on outer-world shamanic tools. I consider what will set the proper stage or mood for the communion—what altar or intention do I want to create, and who and what do I wish to accompany me on the journey? Which colored cloth feels right to place under the sacred objects of the altar? For example, when working with the elements, I will often choose a blue-colored altar cloth for the water cycle, dark green or brown for the earth cycle, red for the fire cycle, sky blue or celebratory colors of gold and silver for the air cycle, and for the spirit cycle, perhaps white, or gentle green and purple pastels. I might place upon the altar elemental representations of animals or mythological figures, statues of gods or goddesses, or items from the natural world such as feathers for air, stones for earth, candles for fire, and flowers in a vase of water to bring in both water and spirit.

For instance, if I am ready to work with the dissolving nature of the water cycle, I might create an altar and bring in Buddha, who knows how to sit in silence dissolving all illusions; or Kuan Yin, the goddess of unconditional love; or the Egyptian god Osiris, who represents the regeneration of life through the surrender of that which no longer serves us, allowing its dissolution in the waters. Sea creatures like the dolphin, whale, seahorse, or mermaid speak to us of the messages in water and can be allies on the altar.

For earth, I might bring in Terra, the Roman goddess; or Gaia, the Greek personification of earth. I might add the Egyptian god Geb, to represent earth; the Greek goddess Demeter, to represent fertility and the harvest; Artemis, lady of the beasts; and the Egyptian goddess Hathor and god Khnum, for grounding, nurturing our bodies, planting the gardens, and creating new forms. I could also include earthy creatures who teach us to either slow down and become methodical, or to seek out and be aware of the path ahead, and who aid us in creating purposeful and forward-moving earth steps—such as the sloth, dog, bear, earthworm, prairie dog, or elephant.

For the fire element, the Roman goddess Vesta, who tends to the fires of hearth and home, might offer support to a person who has a lot of fire and needs to learn how to wield it purposefully and carefully. Or, if one needs to gather more fire for action, the goddess Sekhmet might be appropriate, as she helps us to get through the birth canal, and her fires purify and burn off that which we no longer need in life. Animals such as snakes, large cats, serpents, or dragons commonly represent fire.

For the air element we might call on Athena, the Greek goddess of wisdom, since wisdom is a characteristic of the air element. Venus, the Roman goddess of higher love and wisdom, and the Egyptian god Horus, the falcon-headed deity who sees the bigger picture in the air realm, can help us in giving concrete form to air's inspirations. I often bring in birds as animal allies for the air element, especially the high flyers such as the condor, eagle, or hawk, as they are the ones who bring messages and inspiration from the upper realms of spirit down to earth through the air currents.

To support the spirit cycle, I may call on Jesus, or the ancient goddess Inanna; the ones who know how to surrender fully to spirit. I might also include archangels, saints, or companions of the angelic realm, as well as fairies, dragonflies, or butterflies. All these help us connect to the divine essence of our soul as well as the Great Mystery beyond time and space. These are just a few suggestions to stimulate your creativity and augment your experience of connecting with each element.

Further Shamanic Exploration: Being with Nature, to Know Your Own Nature

As we grow and expand in our nature, as we embrace our "humane-ity," we will need to embrace all the elements—water, earth, fire, spirit, and air—to be whole and vital beings. We can know where we are deficient relative to the elements, and that although we do not have to carry all with equal proportion, it serves us to cultivate a relationship with them all. Some of us will naturally do more airy things, fiery things, earthy things, or watery things, yet we can each use our strengths to support one another and our collective dreams. Carl Jung said we all have a certain amount of these elemental qualities. He called them the four psychological functions: thinking (air), feeling (water), sensation (earth), and intuition (fire); and we express these functions in either introverted or extroverted ways.

Unlike past generations, today's young people do not have to wait as long to know themselves in this way and to understand their world. They have the opportunity to branch out and explore from a younger age, and therefore to understand their strengths and weaknesses as well as which elements they naturally inhabit. So if you discover that your strong suit is air and fire, like mine, great! Be a rider on the storm, create, burn it up, and become a catalyst in the lives of others. If you want to stay the same, I'm not your gal. I will, however, get my own and your butt through the birth canal if you want it. I am a great spiritual midwife. Part of this skill comes from understanding my own weaknesses, which lie in the water and earth elements. I have to work at cultivating those aspects within myself, or surround myself with those elements either in nature or in watery or earthy people, to balance out the fire and air in my own nature.

The uninitiated play to their strengths, only and always. The initiated says, "I will continue to cultivate and flourish in my strengths, but I will develop humility and seek out those elements and people with contrasting strengths, and say, "Teach me!" I will not say, "Bad water, bad earth," and harbor a grudge against watery people or earthy people. This is why wars begin, because uninitiated human beings cannot see the strength and value of "the other" who is different from them. The would-be initiate must become more adept with every part of the elemental wheel, but that means first knowing where our place on the wheel lies.

The air and fire elements are easy for me to embrace and feel free and nurtured by. My wounds are with what some have deemed to be the more feminine elements of water and earth, not the masculine elements. I have had healthy relationships with many men in my life in a variety of roles. I have even facilitated men's groups and never felt intimidated. My learning curve, to be fully initiated, has been to connect with the watery, earthy feminine. For years in my thirties and forties, I ran women's groups and priestess groups because I needed to connect with the feminine. I needed to learn about the feminine. I come by that nature from my lineage; like me, my mother is very yang, or more masculine in nature. In the small southern Kentucky town I grew up in, many of the women were more yang than yin; they had to be to survive. My mom has been a hard worker throughout her life, and at ninety-three she is still alive and managing to live in her home with some family support. She was the primary caregiver to my dad, who passed away a few years ago after having dementia the last couple of years. He couldn't have picked a better, or tougher, person to have by his side. I was very sensitive as a child, so I often felt hurt by my mom's seeming lack of sensitivity over the years. Now, as an adult, I can appreciate her ability to make it through anything, and how it taught me to survive many difficulties along the way. That doesn't erase some of the dysfunctional aspects of my upbringing. Nonetheless, I now appreciate, honor, and love my mother more than ever, because I needed that strength and resilience to get through the difficult periods in my life, including the pain I went through several years ago with Brad Collins, my beloved husband and soulmate who passed from this world after his two-year grueling journey with cancer.

So, my strengths lie in fire and air, my areas of expertise . Water and earth remain my harder teachers, the elements from which I continue to learn, drawing them forth within myself. It's essential for us to recognize our strong suits and understand what brings us joy. Myself, I am happiest in the air element, dreaming and visioning alongside others. At times I picture my body, mind, and spirit as being filled with countless tiny "imaginal cells"—a term initially coined by scientists studying butterfly metamorphosis, but that I like to use as a metaphor. I envisage these cells as resembling the body's physical cells, yet each one is a microcosm of my shamanic power of imagination. When I channel the air element, I can visualize these cells awakening and glowing with light, fueling that spiritual power.

And of course, I love the fire element as well, to dance and create and live passionately. But much of my personal growth has come from being an apprentice to water and earth. That's why I moved to North Carolina, to be in the oldest mountains, to be with the wise earth element. When I asked for guidance about where to move when I was ready to leave California, the divine wise ones must have said, "We've got our hands full with this one! Where can we send her? Send her to one of the oldest mountain ranges in the world, to the wooded forests, amid the wild plants and animals, where the waters run down the cascading falls and spill out into the rivers and lakes. She needs all this to be close to earth and water." Indeed, they were right. The land and the waters that surround my Western North Carolina sanctuary/retreat nourish me toward wholeness. They help channel all the inspired and creative forces within me, so I can be of planetary service without burning myself out.

One of the most powerful ways to sync up with the elemental teachers is to go be with them in nature. Sometimes the weather outside can actually bring you into harmony with a particular element. For instance, as we prepare to more deeply explore the water element in the next segment of this chapter, imagine a day on which you have all kinds of plans and activities arranged for yourself, but when you wake up, you find it is a cloudy, rainy day. Suddenly you feel more like curling up with a good book and a cup of tea rather than doing the more earthy or fiery tasks of the day. When we can feel the energy of a day like that and surrender to the larger archetypal pattern, we often find ourselves nourished and rested, which allows us to be more effective at our tasks the next day. If, on the other hand, we are still operating in a more linear model, we might feel depressed by the rain squashing our plans, or frustrated that we can't find the inner fire to make things happen as we wanted. On the spiral path, embracing a "this or something better" approach, and taking life one day at a time, are key skills we must cultivate. If we stay present, commit to the reality of each day, and release rigid expectations, we often end up receiving what we truly need, beyond the ego's desires.

Being with and of the Water

In the waters, we allow ourselves to dissolve away any blockage that is keeping us from moving into the next cycle—all that we have taken on as adults that separates us from playfulness, innocence, and trust. The water is also a place of deep rest, nourishment, and replenishment. You can cultivate your relationship with the water element by physically being with and in the water. Visit the ocean, seek out a river or waterfall on a hike, or go to a fountain in the middle of the city. We can also simply take a shower or bath and become conscious of the way our busy thoughts and to-do lists dissolve away as we let the warm waters caress our skin. When we let ourselves sit in this dissolution long enough, we often find that we have dissolved what needed to be let go, and new and inspired thoughts show up. We find a creativity that our ego mind and agenda may have kept bound up and inaccessible.

We can also access the water element by listening to sound recordings of ocean waves crashing, rainfall dancing on a tin roof, or the bubbling of a river. This can help when we feel overly energized and need to settle our energy down in order to focus, sleep, or relax. Or we may choose to engage with the watery environment through meditation, or immersion into a "sensory deprivation" float tank. If we feel we need a prolonged experience of the water to balance out a fiery nature within, we might paint the walls in our home or hang pictures to help us feel surrounded by watery landscapes, colors, and nurturing energies, or we might wear watery-colored clothes, such as deep blue, pastel green, or light purple. On the other hand, you may have an excess of the water element in your innate being, and you might need to bring into your life and environment more of the colors and characteristics of the earth or fire elements, which can encourage you to take action more effectively.

Walking with the Earth

To engage in a deeper relationship with the earth cycle, you might visit a beach. Bury your feet in the sands and feel the warmth of the sun-baked crystals, then visualize grounding yourself by extending roots from your feet deep into the earth, anchoring your physical form. If a beach isn't accessible, a mini sand garden or mandala can serve as a conduit to earth energy; you can use a little rake to move around the grains of sand, with each stroke of the rake deepening your connection to the earth.

As another exercise, go to a meadow and lie upon a large rock with your eyes closed, and listen to that wise old rock-being as it shares its wisdom. Feel how it supports the weight of your body and rises up to meet you in physical form. Notice how gravity connects you to this solid being who knows something of patient growth and development over a long period of time.

Or perhaps you could make a trip to the mountains, climb to the top, and look out upon the endless vista of life below. Feel how the mountains have withstood the violent upheavals from the core of the Earth to rise to these great heights and gain perspective, even as the elements of water, fire, and air impact their surfaces. Yet they persist, with their rock faces eroded by the waters, their soils transported by the winds, and their skins purified by the fires. They understand the process of change and how nature takes its course in seasonal and cyclical fashion. They can help us remain grounded while still allowing for and trusting in life's transformations.

You might go to a cave and allow the sheltered, quiet space to hold you as you hibernate, sitting quietly and contemplating what is ready to die within you, so that you may spiral along the path to the next cycle. Ask yourself, what do I need to release before I can take the actions that are necessary at this time?

If you can't climb to a mountaintop, bring the mountain's essence to you by meditating with stones like obsidian, known for its grounding energy and capacity to facilitate cord cutting, or the severing of outdated patterns and energies, which is especially useful in navigating and transforming toxic or codependent relationships. This doesn't always mean ending the relationship, but rather altering its dynamics.

Cultivating a garden, whether large or small, is another profound way to connect with Earth's cycles. A garden teaches us the essentials of growth: providing nutrient-rich soil for our dreams to root, understanding the patience needed for germination, and offering the care required for new sprouts to withstand nature's challenges. It shows us the right time to harvest and the importance of allowing a period of dormancy, ensuring that with each new spring, our growing plants will have the strength and vigor to push up through the soil once again.

If we recognize ourselves as a microcosm of the garden, attuned to nature's cycles, we realize that experiencing life's various stages repeatedly is a necessity for our growth. Immersing our hands and feet in the garden soil connects us viscerally to these primal rhythms.

Dancing with the Fire

From earth cycle's place of stability, planting seeds, and plotting our steps forward, we now take the leap into the fire element, the place of strong will and right action. If we are not prepared to enter the locus of fire and action, we might unwittingly slip back into the earth cycle and get stuck there. Of all the elements, I find that people have the strongest reactions to fire. They love its warmth, comfort, and life-giving nature, but at the same time, they can deeply fear its power.

As humans, we understand instinctively that this element, of all the elements, has allowed our species to evolve itself. The control of fire was a turning point in human cultural evolution. Fire provided warmth, protection, and a method for cooking food. These advancements allowed for our ancestors' geographic dispersal, cultural innovations, and changes to diet and behavior. Additionally, harnessing fire allowed the expansion of human activity into the dark and cold hours of the morning and night. We therefore have a primal understanding that the one who holds the power of fire will prevail and survive. The fire element, linked to our personal will, calls us to elevate our intentions toward collective well-being rather than self-serving goals, channeling our creativity for the greater good.

Fire is the only element that does not exist on its own. It initially had to be discovered and then had to be sparked into existence each time it was needed. To maintain fire requires action; it needs sticks to feed it, and the air must be present to fan its flames, and the water and earth are necessary to tamp it down when the flames grow out of control. Fire is the most magical and powerful element, yet it is also the most dependent, requiring the attention of all the other elements in order to be its most creative self and to sustain and direct its power. In these ways, fire is the essence of alchemy. It is the element of ultimate transformation, and this power lives within the heart and soul of each human being.

In the dance of elements, water facilitates our dissolution and rebirth, earth is where we plant the seeds of new endeavors, and fire, rightly harnessed, nurtures growth and fruition. Managing the fire element in our lives calls for an alignment of will, dedication, and careful attention, respecting both its life-giving warmth and its potential to consume. A master of this balance is an alchemist, capable of profound internal change and of inspiring transformation in others. Fire symbolizes passion and creativity as well as anger and destruction. Engaging with fire responsibly demands a deep appreciation for its dual nature and a commitment to reconciling these forces. At times fire must be allowed to destroy and cleanse, to make way for fresh starts, in the same way a natural wildfire rejuvenates a forest. This regenerative destruction makes room for new life, freeing space from the old and the stagnant. Thus the true skill of the alchemist and the shaman lies in knowing how to utilize the element of fire for the greater good, and guiding its strength to serve creation's continuous cycle.

The shaman, coming from a place of love, has the wisdom to understand that rage and fury are merely the destructive flames of passion and creativity that have not yet found a life-giving, regenerative purpose and outlet for expression. In other words, rage is the result of an untended fire. The creativity, passion, and life-giving sexual energy in a person has not been given the nourishment and direction to grow steadily and to be expressed in a healthy way. The air and space to fan the flames appropriately have not been provided, and healthy boundaries from the earth and water have not been set. All these tools are needed to allow creativity and passion to flourish within a structured and safe container. Rage can feel frightening and destructive. Culturally we tend to either use that power to our advantage—if operating as a bully from a place of insecurity, arrogance, or selfish advancement—or we hide away our anger, and with it our creativity, in our fear of hurting others. If we are unable to find our spark and to welcome the warmth of intimacy, passion, and creativity into our hearts, we either lash out or we fade away.

If we do not fully comprehend fire's role within us, we may suppress our inner turmoil with harmful habits or outer-world distractions. Similarly, fearing the external expression of our rage, we might direct it inward, potentially falling into depression and seeking solace in addiction or medication.

So, to be a shaman is to master the alchemy of fire, harnessing sexual energy to fuel our dreams and our creative force. We must steward our power responsibly, not fear it. Unexpressed, this potent energy may manifest in harmful outbursts, but when channeled with intention, it becomes a force for positive transformation.

How do we learn to channel this element in a positive way? We might first consider that because it is such a powerful force, even an innocent misstep could cause someone to get burned. It might be tempting to shut down the fire in these situations, but the true shaman understands that forgiveness was co-created along with fire. Whether such accidents happen with an actual fire or within our relationships, the shaman remains humble and makes amends, but keeps their inner fire alive nonetheless, living and learning.

Embracing the Aquarian Shaman within involves igniting our inner passion and connecting to the life force energy, located at the base of the spine, that is known in Hinduism as Kundalini life force. It's about taking risks and engaging with potent energies for growth. As we navigate this power, we learn to make amends for unintended consequences. We do not apologize for who we are, but for the fallout of our growth process as we learn to wield the power of gods—the power of creation itself. Shamans recognize the necessity of fire's destructive power, seeing potential in the ashes for rebirth. In shamanism, no element is purely good or bad; what may seem catastrophic to the ego can be fertile ground for regeneration of the shaman's soul.

Engaging with the fire element demands vigilant focus to prevent the flames from either being extinguished or raging uncontrolled. To begin to work with this element directly, one can light a candle, or build and tend a fire within a safe vessel. Observe what feeds the fire, what causes the flames to rise up or die down. Watch how the flames dance in an erratic, creative fashion. Feel the warmth of the flames upon your skin, and listen to the crackle as the fire burns through paper and wood. Observe the fire's response to the wind's whistle and how a gentle blow revives the embers, sparking the flames back to life with just a breath. Also notice your own feelings about the fire. Does it feel fun and powerful, or onerous and threatening? What qualities do you already share with this fire, and what new ways of being might it unveil to you?

Cooking can be a practical way to commune with the fire element. It teaches us that insufficient heat leaves food undercooked, not reaching its potential, while too much heat leads to a charred, inedible result. Similarly, we need the right amount of transformative fire to become our best selves; too little and we're underdeveloped, too much and we risk burnout. If you're feeling emotionally overcooked, it's beneficial to seek rejuvenation in more soothing elements before igniting your creative flames once more.

A more indirect, yet powerful way to explore fire is through dance. It awakens the Kundalini energy at the spine's base, propelling it upward like a serpent, invigorating our sexual and creative energy and igniting our soul's passion. Notice how dancing makes you feel: Does it liberate and energize you, or do you feel too inhibited and uncomfortable to lose yourself in the dance? Your response can reveal your affinity with the fire element and may encourage you to explore beyond your comfort zone.

One last note on fire. According to alchemical legend, fire is crucial to the process of turning metal into pure gold. It is also required, along with a great deal of pressure, to transform a lump of coal into a glittering diamond. What raw material in your life could metamorphose into gold or a diamond if you fanned your inner flames? What lights your fire? What turns your heart on?

Freedom in the Spirit

When we enter the spirit cycle, we move into the element of ether, and into surrender. In nature, spirit is less about a physical place and more about a state of connecting to love and trust. After the fires of purification have burned away any ego residue that keeps us from connecting with true, authentic, divine love, we move into the element of spirit. In this evolution on the spiral path, we turn over our personal will to divine will. This is the point of the birthing process at which we stop all the pushing of the fire cycle, and surrender to imminent birth, knowing we have done our part and there is nothing more we can do. We are now merely the love-filled vessel for the miraculous.

In the spirit element, we gather up all our most heartfelt dreams, place them on the altar of our lives, and offer everything up to love, with the invocation, "Let thy will become my will." We trust that we have done what was needed at this point on the journey to make ourselves a pristine vessel for creation, and we release any expectations for exactly how or in what ways our dreams will come to pass. We say a prayer to all in this universe that loves us: "Please, Creator/Co-creator, bring me this or something better. Thank you." In this way, we can move forward in taking action in service of our dream with a faith that what is co-created will be for the highest good, regardless of how it turns out or what our ego might say about it. When we surrender our dreams to the altar, we trust that if the answer "no" comes back, it doesn't signify a personal failure on our part; it only means that this dream is not meant for us at this time, and something better is in store. Spirit is a cycle in which we have released ego attachment to outcome.

The route to accessing the spirit cycle is first and foremost a question of how to enter our hearts. When we enter our hearts and our lives through love, we have wisdom. In the heart we do not make a choice about whether to think or feel; rather, we undergo a both/and experience, thinking and feeling. The heart is the place of integration where we pull up all the human feelings and emotions from the lower energy centers, and also pull down the thinking mind from the upper energy centers. In the heart, the seat of the soul, the human body and spirit are merged in an alchemical stew. From this place in which love and wisdom unite, we can see both what has been and what is coming. We feel calm and relaxed in this perspective, because as humans we have done what we needed to do, and the rest is up to something greater than ourselves. It is the calm before the rebirth; we feel supported, and we trust the process.

An effective way to engage with the spirit cycle is through music—with its ethereal frequencies, it resonates with the spirit element by touching our souls and opening our hearts. There is a wonderful song by Sting called "Whenever I Say Your Name." I imagine as I listen to the words that the one who is being courted in this song is our higher power, our inner beloved, and the song is offering a prayer and invocation to the one who co-creates with us—particularly through these few lyrics:

> *Whenever your memory feeds my soul, whatever got broken becomes whole*
> *Whenever I'm filled with doubts that we will be together*
> *Wherever I lay me down, wherever I put my head to sleep*
> *Whenever I hurt and cry, whenever I got to lie awake and weep*
> *Whenever I kneel to pray, whenever I need to find a way*
> *I'm calling out your name*
> *Whenever those dark clouds hide the moon*
> *Whenever this world has gotten so strange*
> *I know that something's gonna change*

Celebrating in the Air

The air is a space around and within us. Air is the breath of God entering our bodies and fueling the flames of our fire and passion. In the air cycle, we open ourselves to all the elements, so they are Kundalini energy running through our bodies without resistance. The air blows upon and kindles all the elements in communion, and this allows all the energy centers to open. Air builds the momentum of all the energies until, through their alignment, rebirth occurs. Shamanic consciousness is awakened, and we can see our soul's full purpose. We have come through the birth, and now we celebrate our freedom from the constraints of the birth canal. With newfound clarity, vision, and zest, we are ready to present our rejuvenated selves to the world at a new level of being.

Engaging with the air cycle in nature, much like witnessing a spontaneous birth, can't be scheduled; wind graces us unexpectedly when conditions align. The winds of change bring an energetic stir, a hint of the powerful force of renewal. By opening our arms to a gust and leaning into it, we can envisage the sensation of flight, embracing the liberty and joy inherent in rebirth. Of course the simplest and most profound way to experience the air cycle is to actively and purposefully engage in breathing, thus allowing the breath to catalyze our transformation and rebirth.

SHAMANIC INTEGRATION EXERCISE
Spiraling to the First Five Sacred Elements Within

We have described the innate qualities of each element and cycle, and discussed how to access and learn from each element. For this section's exercise, contemplate your natural way of being. Take inventory of which elements you feel are especially strong in you, and notice the elements that feel scary or unappealing. List the personality traits you feel you possess that are reflective of specific elements. If making a list feels too rigid and uncomfortable, you might instead draw a circle with different colors for the elements, like a pie chart, indicating how much of each element you feel you naturally possess. Or you could invent your own creative and expressive way to depict the balance of elements within your being.

After this mental inventory, allow yourself to move beyond ego assessment and toward a body-and-soul experience of the elements. Using some of the outer shamanic tools I have mentioned throughout this book, create a sacred space for communion. Explore which inner prayer or meditation resonates with you. There are many paths to commune with the divine that allow us to put the ego aside, opening the way to the divine's presence.

Adopting the role of a supplicant is beneficial when seeking guidance or support. You might make a protective prayer, asking for the insight you need. Find a quiet space to sit or recline, and turn inward with a heartfelt plea such as "Please help, and thank you," echoing the words of Gram Twylah. Breathe deeply in this contemplation, accompanied by silence or music that connects you to the element you're focusing on. Let yourself drift, without agenda, and see what arises. Like Forest Gump saying "life is like a box of chocolates," you, too, can open the box and see which chocolate calls to you, without knowing the flavor of its filling. Take a leap of faith, bite in, and let your body feel the experience without ego judgment. This approach is particularly effective when you're uncertain about your needs or direction. It allows you to delve deeper, explore your inner landscape, and await the emergence of insights or messages.

Another way to connect with the divine and the elements is through affirmation. Ask yourself, "What is up for me right now, and what support do I need at this time?" You may get an answer such as, "I feel I am in the earth cycle letting go of outworn habits. My inner child requires the reassurance of love and safety so I can journey within to reclaim parts of that child that were lost. Then I can make the necessary changes in my outer world." In this case, telling yourself "I am safe and I love myself" can allow you to begin your journey with greater direction and comfort.

Next, to more actively engage in this deep reflection with the elements, you might invoke the knowledge within you in an authoritative manner, calling the support you need toward you. For example, when facing reluctance or fear at the brink of a significant personal milestone, summon the fiery strength of an archetype like Sekhmet. You might say, "Sekhmet, aid me in birthing this new aspect of myself. Help burn away any remnants hindering my passage through the birth canal. I call upon your fiery essence to guide me through fear and into transformation." This proactive invocation empowers your journey, asserting your readiness for change. Each method, whether supplication, affirmation, or invocation, is valid; the choice depends on self-awareness and the necessities of the moment.

Finally, if you are feeling dynamic and seeking an alternative to stillness, a walkabout can be a profound way to connect with the elements. It's a journey of synchronicity in nature, being open to messages from the environment. You might find significance in a stone or stick, or encounter animals that offer insights. Immersing your feet in a stream, lying on a sun-warmed rock, or listening to the wind's secrets, you can engage directly with nature's elements. This method is one of my preferred practices for communing with nature, the elements, the archetypes, and Mother Earth. My walkabouts often evolve into spontaneous rituals honoring ancestral messages or the very essence of nature through prayer, an offering, or my own tears.

When communing with the elements, regardless of method, it's essential to embrace both the divine source and the divine within from a place of gratitude. Our engagement and closure with the sacred are sensed deeply by our own inner divinity and the Great Mystery. Making a prayer or an offering, even a hair off your head, to thank the divine for the gift of wisdom and communion, establishes an equal exchange of energy and respect.

After you've identified how the elements and cycles of change are currently working within you, and practiced communion with the elements and the divine, you might next do an integration activity.

You could journal about your experience: What came to you? How did it come? What parts of the experience do you wish to carry forward? If journaling does not speak to you, use art, dance, or ceremony to bring meaningful closure to your exercise and integrate this newfound understanding into your being.

While the concept may seem complex, engaging with the elemental cycles can be a brief daily practice. Taking twenty to thirty minutes for self-reflection and to identify the energies at play can yield significant insights. For those who seek deeper connection, forming an elemental study group or pairing with a friend for this journey can enrich the experience. Attending a SHIP workshop can offer another avenue for exploration. However, starting with simple, personal daily check-ins is a powerful step in itself.

16

The Sixth Cycle

Imaginal Cells

The sixth cycle stands apart from the first five cycles of change in that it moves beyond the physical elements of nature into the super-nature, or supernatural; therefore I've given it a chapter of its own. Recall how earlier I encouraged you to envision yourself as being filled with tiny "imaginal cells" that symbolize the power of your shamanic imagination. Close your eyes and picture these imaginary cells becoming activated, thus propelling the Kundalini energy upward like a column of light shining from the crown of your head. See this inner light of creativity uniting with the power of external potential, which in turn infuses your imaginal cells in a feedback loop of electrifying promise. The sixth cycle on the shamanic loop involves visualizing your next phase of growth, merging new possibilities into your being. Having celebrated your recent achievements, you're poised to meet the image of your future self. But to make this new self a reality, you must re-enter the waters of gestation, beginning the cycle once more.

A natural, real-world parallel to the workings of imaginal cells is the humble caterpillar's breathtaking transformation into a butterfly. To observe the imaginal cells cycle in nature, I invite you to study this miraculous phenomenon. Witnessing it firsthand may be rare, so let's explore the caterpillar's journey together here; in doing so, I hope to inspire your awe and connect you with the transformative power of your imaginal cells, guiding you toward your future self as an Aquarian Shaman.

How the Caterpillar Co-creates with the Imaginal Cells to Become a Butterfly

There is nothing in a caterpillar that tells you it's going to be a butterfly.

R. BUCKMINSTER FULLER

Through my Shamanic Breathwork experiences, I've received profound insights about our potential for complete transformation, akin to a caterpillar's metamorphosis into a butterfly—shedding its former self and form. I have a great interest in science, which has only deepened my sense of wonder in divine creation, as scientific findings have now validated many phenomena once dismissed as fanciful.

Several years ago, I received this message from one of our Venus Rising University graduates: "Star Wolf, I think this film by Barbara Marx Hubbard on imaginal cells is exactly what you've been teaching about shamanic transformation and symbolic death and rebirth of our old ego identities!" Naturally I couldn't wait to watch the film, and I was not disappointed.

Barbara Marx Hubbard, a visionary teacher who has since departed our world, illuminated the concept of imaginal cells in her work. This term crystallized what I've been conveying about shamanic death and rebirth; I simply lacked the scientific terminology. "Imaginal cells," a term I initially thought was coined by Hubbard, was actually invented by scientists studying butterfly metamorphosis. It's thrilling to see such a term that bridges science and spirituality, honoring the enigmatic nature of transformation and igniting the imagination. This convergence of science and spiritual understanding is a profound step toward a more integrated perspective of our world.

The caterpillar's journey is an exquisite metaphor for imaginal cells and transformation as an Aquarian Shaman conceives of them. A caterpillar starts out as an unassuming creature, focused solely on consumption, similar to how some human societies engage in consumerism. The caterpillar eats voraciously, can double its size in a single day, and seems to take more from nature than it gives back. To an observer unaware of its destiny, the caterpillar might seem like a pest, a representation of unchecked consumption that offers nothing to the earth in return. Yet this stage is crucial, driven by an inner compulsion that is part of a grander scheme. The caterpillar's insatiable appetite mirrors our own human tendency to fill our inner void with material things. It's a reminder that, like the caterpillar, our own periods of consumption may be part of a process, a prelude to our transformation.

At some point in its life, the caterpillar undergoes a dramatic alteration, sparking scientific intrigue. Researchers have delved into this mystery, hypothesizing that an innate evolutionary signal triggers the change when the caterpillar has reached a critical point. Imagine this creature, perhaps pondering its gluttonous indulgence or the dwindling resources it has over-consumed, feeling the onset of an existential crisis as it confronts its vulnerability in a stripped habitat. At this juncture, the imaginal cells within it awaken. The caterpillar, now at its limit, facing potential dangers and predators beyond its leafless refuge, reaches a moment of surrender, ready for a change it can't yet fathom. This pivotal moment encapsulates the profound leap from the mundane to the miraculous, setting the stage for a radical transition beyond the caterpillar's current existence.

As the caterpillar grapples with a profound sense of aimlessness, a void where direction should be, a soft whispering emerges from the depths of its existential quandary. It is the voice of the caterpillar's imaginal cells, urging it toward a branch high above. With no rationale offered, this internal prompt elicits a deep, almost primordial drive within the caterpillar. It musters the last reserves of its energy, battling the inertia that has claimed it, inching with laborious effort toward the perch. This climb, fueled by a mysterious compulsion rather than logic, embodies the leap of faith inherent in nature's cycles: the caterpillar ascends, offering itself to the unknown, propelled by a trust in the process that defies its current understanding.

Upon the tree limb, the caterpillar halts, bereft of comfort and necessities. It questions, "Now what?"—prompting the imaginal cells to guide it and say, "Secrete a liquid, move around a little, then fall apart in a spiral fashion." Obediently, it spins a cocoon—its chrysalis—a tomb for transformation, a womb for rebirth. "Chrysalis" is a shamanic word that refers to transmuting yourself into something entirely new. As the caterpillar spins and swirls itself into a vortex, the Kundalini energy pulses within. The small creature feels utterly spent, yet has an awareness of a greater force at play. Doubts assail its tiny mind, but it yields to trust in the larger cycle.

In the throes of transformation, the caterpillar senses an impetus to crack open its form. The ensuing metamorphosis, likely an incredibly painful process for the small creature, may cause it to doubt its choice, wondering why it didn't remain on the ground below, where it was happy in its life as a caterpillar. Yet it knows, if it is fully honest with itself, that its old mode of being was no longer working. It would have died down there, easy pickings for a hungry bird. Stagnation in comfort is certain demise. To embrace the unknown means placing oneself in potential danger, but also signifies a chance at renewal, a defiant stand against a predestined fate as prey.

Down on the ground, other caterpillars might mock and jeer, casting ridicule on the insect's solitary journey. At this point, the pain and suffering the little creature has endured seem quite cruel, and a sympathetic observer might wish for it to be put out of its misery. Yet its trials are not over. Now, the last vestiges of who and what the creature was, its former identity, begin to secrete acidic goo that eats away the rest of its being, disintegrating it completely. The caterpillar endures, its essence dissolving into a primordial soup—a spectacle of true alchemy. Its eyeballs fall out, its tail falls off, its legs fall off, and it turns into caterpillar mush. Sometimes I'll say, "I feel like caterpillar mush today"—my way of expressing that some part of myself as I knew it has broken apart, and though it is painful at the moment, I know it opens a door to a new beginning.

During this pivotal stage, the caterpillar becomes a visceral emblem of "nigredo," an alchemical term for the deepest darkness preceding transformation. Here, it simmers in potentiality, at the very nadir of its existence, teetering between the finality of physical death and the profound shedding of its former self. It is a crucible moment, where all that's left is the threshold of utter dissolution or the genesis of rebirth. This stark juncture in the caterpillar's journey mirrors our own dark night of the soul, where the only way out is through—a passage that leads either to the cessation of being or to a profound metamorphosis.

In this transformative limbo, the once-caterpillar is on the cusp of the unimaginable. Here, in the depths of uncertainty, the whispers of the imaginal cells beckon—an energy field of potential that enshrouds this being, murmuring the secrets of metamorphosis. This is the crux of alchemy where, amidst the chaos of disintegration, the possibility of rebirth is illuminated. As the creature stews in its own dissolution, the imaginal cells—long suffused in its environment, unnoticed like water to a fish—begin their work. It's a profound realization that scientists have had, watching caterpillars undergo this process: Transformation doesn't arise solely from the caterpillar itself, but out of a dialogue with invisible, surrounding forces, the energy field of the imaginal cells. The caterpillar's journey is cradled by a larger, cosmic intelligence that urges, "Climb the tree, encircle yourself in the spiral, surrender to the void, and emerge anew." Our own lives echo this pattern; often, it's only when we're unraveled by life's trials that we become permeable to the spirit world, receptive to the whispers of change that prompt us toward rebirth.

Within the chrysalis, the caterpillar undergoes profound transformation, guided invisibly by the imaginal cells. This process is a stark reminder of life's solitary journeys, and offers a lesson of particular importance to those with codependent tendencies. If we give in to the temptation to intervene, to snip open the cocoon and alleviate the nascent butterfly's struggle, we inadvertently cripple its development. The internal battle within the chrysalis ultimately strengthens the butterfly's wings, granting it the power to fly. Thus, we must hold in check our impulse to rescue, honoring the sacred struggle that gifts others—and ourselves—with flight-worthy wings. Each being must wrestle with its own chrysalis, emerging when it alone has mustered the strength to face the skies.

So, then, let's assume we do not interrupt this little being's process. The butterfly has been created, and birth is now imminent. In this moment we might imagine a halo of light around this being, a golden, divine glow that emerges from the darkness.

Let's shape-shift briefly and ourselves become that butterfly. Like the imaginal cells that help the caterpillar forward in its journey, our own bodies and spirits have the ability to use shamanic imagination to tell us when it is time to grow and transform. When we first arrive out of our cocoon, we may be shaken up, even unsure of our identity. We are like a human baby who emerges for the first time into the world, perhaps drugged and foggy-headed from the hospital birth process, with blurry vision, our eyes unaccustomed to the bright light. As our vision adjusts, we see a new reality. We may notice our hands and wonder if they will hurt us, and we have a profound sense of needing something, though we don't yet know what it is. In the end we try crying, thinking that if we cry, perhaps the large, strange creatures around us will bring something to make us feel better. In this way, we make new discoveries and are in awe at the magic of the unknown.

Let us return to the butterfly. It has gone through the birth process and now must stretch himself and get his bearings. Perhaps he wonders what has happened to his feet and his tail. Yet as he is moving his strange new body, his wings unfold! A soft breeze blows, and without yet knowing what the wings are for, and feeling off-balance in the wind, his first instinct is to fold them back up again. We humans may do the same, in attempting something new—we will try it for a little while and it feels good, but then our new power begins to scare us, and we may attempt to sabotage our own progress.

Yet as the butterfly's former caterpillar friends look on, some with envy, some with awe, an inner force spurs him to take a leap and, to his surprise, he flies! This metamorphosis sparks a ripple of wonder among the onlookers, challenging their beliefs and stirring questions within them about their own potential for change and growth.

As the butterfly soars through the sky, it occurs to him that he wishes to give back to the world, in exchange for this incredible new life he has been granted. So when he grows hungry and flutters down onto a flower to nourish himself, he pollinates that flower. Every flower he visits, every plant he lands upon, he brings new life to. There is now a natural exchange between this being and the beauty of the world. He receives, and in receiving he gives back. No longer is he the caterpillar, driven solely by consumption, eating everything in his vicinity; instead, each plant from which he eats grows fuller and healthier, and new plants are seeded all through his habitat.

How beautiful it is to watch, this transfiguration from a place of despair, through which his imaginal cells supported him, giving him the courage to die and be reborn so he could ultimately be of service to the planet, nourishing himself through equal exchange of energy and abundance.

"Ye shall know them by their fruits"; "Man doth not live by bread only, but by every word that proceedeth out of the mouth of the Lord doth man live"—every spiritual tradition contains some form of these teachings. This exquisite creature, the butterfly, brings light and beauty to the world. He feeds and gives back. And, incredibly, if he is a monarch butterfly, he says, "I believe in myself; I think I'll take a trip to South America!" He flies 2000 to 3000 miles, along with millions of other butterflies. Remember, this is a being whose wings are so thin that you can see through them. Yet millions of monarch butterflies successfully make this journey every year, landing at the tree of their ancestors, though they've never visited it before in physical form. They undergo a pilgrimage to this ancient homeland, guided by nothing more than their imaginal cells.

So, I ask you, if the humblest creature can be a teacher to us humans, with all our creative brilliance, what can we do? What can we dream? Suddenly, a big life change like a move across the country doesn't feel so daunting. We do not have to grow wings; we do not have to hang from a tree limb and build a cocoon. We have to embrace transformation in our own way, but compared to the trials of the butterfly, the challenges we face appear quite manageable.

☙☙

SHAMANIC EXERCISE
Connect with Your Imaginal Cells

Close your eyes for a minute. Reflect on a time when you knew absolutely that you'd transmuted your caterpillar self into a butterfly and done something you'd previously thought impossible. As a caterpillar you never would have attempted it, but as a butterfly you did! Perhaps it was the accomplishment of a daunting goal, or a change in habit or behavior. Let yourself remember and appreciate all it took to birth yourself into that new way of being.

With your eyes still closed, take several deep and full breaths, and imagine you are encircled by imaginal cells. They can appear in any way you want—bubbles, sparkles, seashells, vibrations and frequencies, even real cells dividing. Imagine them speaking to you. Feel their touch, like feathers brushing your skin, or perhaps crystalline grains of sand, or raindrops, or currents in the air. Imagine they are all waiting, right now, for you to turn your life over to their keeping. They will not steer you wrong. Their only mission is to help you evolve into whoever your heart is longing to be. As you use this exercise to expand your shamanic imagination, you might feel hot and cold, jittery with life force energy and Kundalini.

After you have been with these feelings and sensations, slowly come back to your present moment. You might draw or paint, dance or sing, or journal about your experiences of future destiny. Now ask yourself, "What am I ready and willing to do to manifest something new in my life?"

SHAMANIC EXPERIENCES FOR A QUANTUM SHIFT

17

Accelerated Transformation through Shamanic Breathwork

Having now fully explored working with the elements, the cycles of change, and how we move through transformation, we will venture into a quantum shamanic experience, working with all the alchemy of change within your cellular nature through the Shamanic Breathwork Process. It is the most effective "inner shamanic tool" I have found for accelerating shamanic consciousness and transformation.

I can remember a much younger me, tearfully confessing to my teacher one rainy afternoon that I felt I was a complete failure at committing to just one spiritual path, as so many of my friends had done at that time. She asked me to share more of what was ailing me, and I shamefully told her I simply couldn't seem to commit to one form of religion or spirituality. I felt that perhaps I lacked discipline. I sobbed and lamented that I had been a peace-and-love hippie, a Baptist, a Catholic, a Buddhist, a Goddess worshiper, a New Ager, and a vegetarian. I had studied and taught Helen Schucman's *A Course in Miracles*, attended countless twelve-step meetings, worked as a traditional mental health professional, and later moved on to working in holistic care.

At this point in my confession, a smile moved slowly across my teacher's face as she gently laughed out loud, and offered words that resonated with my soul: "You aren't doing anything wrong. You're like me; you're on the path of direct experience." She called me a "body pilot," or in other words, one whose purpose is to embody many different experiences and teachings, to know them firsthand in an intimate, direct way. By integrating these varied experiences into my life and human form, I would be led to an inner knowing of the deeper origins of all these outer teachings. Never has anything felt truer to me than this summation of my purpose. My teacher was not a flatterer; if I had been truly off course, she would have told me so. Thus, I felt my heart releasing the self-judgment and shame I had long carried.

It was at this point that I began to consciously co-create what I would later call the Shamanic Breathwork Process, and ultimately SHIP—my own version of external teachings that I integrated with my deeper awakening of my Aquarian Shaman on the path of direct experience.

Shamanic Breathwork journeying is the primary method or inner shamanic tool that I utilize myself on the spiral path, and also the primary modality I use to support others through my training and shamanic initiations programs. Shamanic Breathwork is a powerful process that is often enhanced by group dynamics and group sharing; however, it can also be undertaken independently at home. On a spiritual journey we are never truly alone, even if we are the only one physically in the room. That is why I've spent so much time in this book discussing how to establish a sacred space, where those beings from beyond that love us can come to support our Earth walk and spiritual sojourns. Thus, while group dynamics can amplify energy, profound transformations can occur individually during Shamanic Breathwork. Personal intention is powerful. You can simply lie down, focus, enter a sacred mindset, play evocative music, and allow your breath to guide you into deep self-exploration.

If after doing Shamanic Breathwork on your own, you see a benefit in doing so with outside support and possibly with a group of kindred spirits, you might consider attending a Venus Rising retreat at Dove Mountain to participate in one of our accelerated trainings or with an authorized Venus Rising facilitator somewhere around the globe, and there are many. For now, I will detail how you can use this tool to access the inner shaman on your own, in your private sacred space.

Shamanic Breathwork is a highly experiential, ceremonial process that uses deep, circular breathing combined with chakra-attuned music to stir up, activate, and liberate energy held in the chakras, or energy centers, of your being. You can imagine a chakra as a portal between your energy field and your body-felt experience. For instance, you may feel a sensation of butterflies in your stomach when you're nervous, or you may become sick to your stomach when you feel anxious. In other words, when your third chakra is either overstimulated or blocked, this portal to your solar plexus—which connects with your stomach, pancreas, and liver—can cause discomfort in those organs. This can be an indicator that something needs our attention. When we can bring our breath to that place and allow for a release or recognition of the energy sitting there, we are liberated and can allow new, balanced energy to flow in that region.

Playing evocative music that viscerally ignites and is designed to attune to the frequency of each chakra can proactively open and release, or harmonize, each chakra, which allows us to find balance throughout our being. In this way, we are also able to access memories or trauma that may have been stored in these places for many years. Often we have no conscious recollection of these events, but they nonetheless impact our way of experiencing life, and therefore can unconsciously affect our choices and behavior until we bring them to full awareness. To illuminate that which is shrouded from our conscious mind is to proactively engage parts of ourselves that need healing, balance, stimulation, or nurturing. We might view this illumination of that which is concealed from us as a way of working with or dancing with our shadow. In these hidden, shadowy places, we not only find the denser energies that unconsciously influence our choices and behaviors, we also find the biggest, best, and brightest parts of ourselves that we may have hidden away at a young age in response to our childhood environment.

The combination of using our inhalation to bring vitality deeply into our bodies, using a powerful exhale to release tension, and adding musical frequencies to open our energetic and cellular natures, leads to an altered state of consciousness in which the ego and busy "monkey mind" can step aside and allow for your higher knowing to access your entire being, bringing you to a body-felt, direct shift in perception and experience.

It is important to be aware, especially if you are doing this at home alone, that at all times you will innately maintain an awareness—what I term your "witness self"—that keeps you safe even as you journey to unexplored parts of your being. The beauty of this method is that unlike altered states attained through substances, your own wisdom is aware and on board as a filter for how fully you open yourself to the process. In other words, your deeper guidance will only let in what you are able to handle at any given time, and only that which serves your highest good.

As the musical journey begins, you will notice that the music starts off as rhythmic and sometimes percussive, with a deep bass component to stimulate the lower chakras that are more connected to our human body. Progressively, the sounds become more ethereal, peaceful, and gentle to activate the upper chakras that link to our spirit body. Allow yourself to feel the flow of the music and not get caught up in questioning what the music means or what it's doing. The music will generally last about an hour as it moves through all the energy fields. Usually, in a group session, a guided meditation will precede the Shamanic Breathwork experience in order to encourage deeper relaxation. A drum is used during the meditation to sync with the rhythm of the heartbeat, and to inform your psyche that when it hears this drum again at the end of the music, it will be time to return from your journey. If you are home alone, the drum is not essential; you will simply need to bring yourself back to the present when the music stops by taking several deep inhales, then fully exhaling the breath so your body feels the air moving through it strongly and consciously once again. If you own a drum, you might want to drum a bit when you return from your breathwork, to bring yourself back to your body and ground yourself in present time.

When you have completed the breathwork, you may wish to draw or journal to express your experience. Allow yourself to remain in a place of softness, playing heartwarming music that has actual lyrics, which will help you return to the room where you're sitting. Strictly instrumental music can keep you in a more altered state, so it's best to avoid that while working to ground your journey in your body. You also might feel a desire to dance as a way to integrate your experience.

As you bring your breathwork to a close, remember to thank the guides and helpers who were with you on the journey. Make sure to drink plenty of water and eat grounding and nourishing foods, especially root vegetables and protein. An Epsom salt bath or a walk in nature can also be helpful methods to integrate and ground yourself.

Likewise, discussing your journey with a trusted friend can be beneficial. It's common to experience intense emotions or confusion about memories after journeying in this way. Embrace and express your feelings; they are not definitive truths, but rather emotional responses that need to be liberated. Suppressed emotions often cause additional harm, so it's always better to acknowledge and healthily process them.

Be sure to get plenty of rest after journeying. It is best to avoid filling your schedule with outer-world tasks immediately after your Shamanic Breathwork. In the days ahead, you might continue to write in your journal, since the unfolding process will offer further insights and valuable reflections from your experience. I hope, from my heart to yours, that your journey will fulfill your heart's quest and resonate with your soul's deepest yearnings.

18

Quantum Co-creation in Shamanic Communities

For where two or three are gathered together in my name,
there am I in the midst of them.

MATTHEW 18:20 (KJV)

Over thirty years ago in my little hometown in Western Kentucky, I looked around and tried to find people who were my tribe and kindred souls. I had a few dear friends there, but mostly I felt out of place. I was working at the hospital and mental health center, and I also counseled clients in private practice. There were kindhearted people in the town, but only a handful of kindred spirits that I could consider my true community. In fact if I revealed much of myself, I became labeled negatively. At that time, the ministers of the town were all men, but in truth, given the particular type of religion they preached and practiced, it probably wouldn't have mattered if they were male or female. Rather than their gender, it was their dogmatic belief system that led them, at one of their monthly meetings, to proclaim me an agent of the devil. They decided they needed to warn those members of their congregations who were my patients and clients. Looking back on the incident today, I can laugh about it, but at the time it was serious—I received multiple death threats. Because I was an advocate for change, accountability, and personal empowerment, I was the enemy, and small-town ignorance can be dangerous on many levels.

During this difficult period of my life, I would go away to be with soul friends, kindred spirits, mentors, and soul family, to nourish and replenish myself and to remember who I truly was—not the projection people placed upon me. However when I would return back to my hometown, I was alone, and it was challenging. It was so hard to hold on to what I'd felt among my community of the heart, when I had no one nearby to share in that love. Grandmother Twylah always said, "If we were supposed to do it alone, Creator would have only made one of us."

Today when I travel home to my beautiful Loveland Mountain Home Sanctuary and Elemental Temples in Western North Carolina, after having facilitated workshops and trainings around the globe, I feel overwhelming joy and gratitude. I am so profoundly supported by my Venus Rising tribe and family, both here and across the world. I have worked hard to consciously co-create safe, sacred places where I stay connected with all kinds of people, either by going to them or having them come to me and my partners, to join in our work with Venus Rising. Still, embracing my true self is a constant journey, every hour of every day, not just in fleeting moments or on special occasions. Looking back at my past, I recall the struggle to maintain my shifts in consciousness, to fend off depression, to avoid succumbing to addictions, and to not feel isolated or overwhelmed by doubt.

My gratitude is immense, especially because of my humble beginnings on my soul's journey, compared to where I am now in all areas of my life. I have been living in a supportive, comfortable, sustainable manner for many years, doing exactly what I love with my beloveds. My colleagues and I have helped thousands of shamanic souls to answer the calling of their imaginal cells in order to birth their Aquarian Shaman and sacred purpose. Some have been ordained as shamanic ministers with Venus Rising Congregations, or with satellite groups authorized to teach some of our curriculum. Many have acquired a college degree that reflects who they are and the path they are on, through our Venus Rising Shamanic Psychospiritual University, the only one of its kind in the United States. This book is my thirteenth published book.

I used to earn $12,000 per year working at a mental health center, raising my young son in a small fundamentalist town, and longing for my true home and kindred spirits who would finally understand me. Though that town was my childhood home, after my Shamanic Grandmother Mammy Jones died when I was twelve years old, I never felt I belonged there. I do not judge my younger self; nevertheless, I am a quantum leap from where I came from, and by working hard at my inward journey, I created a worldwide community that sustains my growth, as I do theirs. The raw truth is that my pain, stemming from feeling like an outcast and being labeled by ignorance as something I was not, fueled my motivation. It drove me to persist, to trust, and to believe in myself and the transformative journey that lay ahead, revealing the swan, the butterfly within me.

I was able to keep pushing forward and growing because I found ways to be with teachers in other places where I could breathe. I traveled to Dahlonega, Georgia, several times a year to be with my beloved breathwork teacher, and to the reservation outside Buffalo, New York, to be with Wolf Clan Grandmother Twylah Nitsch. My kindred friends and family would remind me of who I truly was. It was enough that I could carry that knowledge and hold it close until I could be with them again, even if we were separated for months at a time. This was before cell phones and email, when people still wrote letters and made occasional long-distance phone calls to stay connected.

Grandmother Twylah and Jacquelyn Small, my two main teachers, wrote me letters of encouragement or left phone messages on my answering machine, and these were like manna from heaven. I would tear open a letter and read it dozens of times, then put it on my little altar in my bedroom to be close to me through my dreams. It was all I had to ground me in the world I was creating for myself, apart from what I carried in my heart. So, I urge you to cherish the connections with your heart and soul's tribe and to honor the elder teachers who have held the light of consciousness to hand off to you to now carry forward. Reach out, share contact details, discover where everyone lives. Join forces, create together, and visit each other. If your surroundings lack a supportive community, take the initiative to forge one, or relocate to a place humming with kindred spirits. It's more than essential—it could be lifesaving. And from what I've seen, it truly empowers you to continue making profound shifts and strides in life.

Community comes in many forms: Buddhist communities, group therapy, church communities, even think tanks where intellectuals come together. Contemporary leadership increasingly makes use of collaborative think tanks and methodologies, steering organizations toward a more Aquarian perspective—in other words, a movement away from traditional hierarchies toward co-creation using our individual and group strengths. Nevertheless, I believe it is essential to listen respectfully to the elders in the world who have brought us to this point, and to hear their humble accounts of their victories and losses. This is one of the best ways to learn and grow from elder knowledge as well as our own visions and dreams.

We can't wait around for others to create the new reality—who are the others anyway, if not us? It is our responsibility to co-create it ourselves, together. We must recognize that our salvation does not rest on a single leader, shaman, or guru. We have entered an era that calls for our maturity, our acknowledgment of how our words and actions influence others. It's our duty to ensure these words and actions are constructive. Furthermore we must seek to align with individuals who exhibit honesty and integrity, who have proven to be dependable, and who engage in collaboration with genuine intent.

To reach a place of healthy co-creation with others, we must each offer truly valuable contributions of our own, rather than seeking only to be directed by another. When souls who've committed to doing their inner work gather in a room and unite all their gifts and talents in service of both their individual and collective dreams, we truly can change the world. To become these awakened Aquarian Shamans, we don't need to go toward the light for enlightenment. We need to go to our depths. It is in our depths that our souls become illuminated. The problem isn't an absence of light in the world; instead, what we lack is depth. This scarcity of depth comes from unprocessed relationship struggles, a barrage of unhealthy and manipulative media, a lost art of thinking critically rather than blindly following popular beliefs and fads, and a lack of deep questioning about our purpose on this planet. We must awaken to our personal power and vision, and then find kindred spirits so we may support one another in this larger project of consciously co-creating the world we wish to inhabit.

We must ask ourselves, have we matured enough to wake up to our humane-ity? Imagine an enlightened new world. Consider the possibility that our perceived divisions are illusory, that we've been separated unnecessarily. Humanity has learned valuable lessons about division and difference, and can now move forward from these experiences. It's time for everyone—not just a select few spiritual seekers and visionaries—to embrace enlightenment, unity, and the power of our diversity. This worldview has sometimes been called fifth dimensional consciousness, or, as I term it, shamanic consciousness, in which the oneness of all creation is perceived by all. Our divinity as individuals presents an opportunity to honor and celebrate our differences, which are humanity's strengths. Diversity in talents and gifts is essential for personal, organizational, and global development. Embracing this diversity empowers humanity to act for the collective highest good.

Has humanity now learned enough from the school of woe to enroll in the school of wisdom? Are we ready to engage in conscious practice every day, to remember our future selves and our shamanic, butterfly souls?

19
Sacred Sites
Pilgrimage and Initiation

One of my favorite ways to make quantum shifts with a community is to lead group pilgrimages to sacred sites all over the world. As we will discuss, the power of community is accelerated further by shared activations at these sacred sites. When an individual or group consciously creates sacred space to participate in, sacred ceremonial "activations" (sudden deep energy shifts) are possible and are often felt body and soul experiences.

A pilgrim is one who journeys to foreign or distant lands, often with the intention to connect with a historical, holy, spiritual, or sacred site. A pilgrimage often requires resources of time, money, and effort, and in this way requires sacrifice and devotion. The word "sacrifice" here is not meant to conjure images of suffering and martyrdom; rather, it communicates that a true soul-calling—whether to a place or circumstance—can foster in us a willingness to give up familiar daily comforts, in order to embrace the exquisite and magical mystery toward which our soul, not our ego, is urging us.

A pilgrimage is not intrinsically rooted in rational or logical thinking. We often do not know why we are called to a pilgrimage, but when we are awakened on the shamanic path, our soul guides us toward the location of our next expansion on the transformational journey. For some, the pilgrimage is a calling to ancestral roots from which our recent family history is disconnected, or to a place with known historical significance for our lineage. It may be a place where a person feels they have experienced a past life, which therefore offers a chance to reclaim some lost soul fragment. It may also be a sacred site that is a portal, where ancient and celestial messages are received, enabling us to bring our future selves into the world for planetary service. A pilgrimage, much like a shamanic journey, can be personal, transpersonal, archetypal, and/or future-self oriented in nature.

The power of pilgrimage to sacred sites comes from the historical and ancestral energy held in a particular location as a result of countless years of ritual, sacrifice, battle, survival, and the ways in which former inhabitants connected with nature's elements and with deities of their time. All this history is held energetically by the land—the stone people, the tree people, the waters, the atmospheric particles in the air, and the local people and animals, both past and present. This energy creates a vortex or field that we can enter into as a portal to connect and commune with both the ancient and future wisdom of the sacred site, and with the planet at large. Our DNA remembers the secret codes of ancient energies, the connections to the land animals and ancestors. When we make pilgrimage to these sites, we have body-felt experiences of the mysteries, and a deep sense of awe in the sacred. We are reminded of the depth of connection that our forerunners had with Mother Nature, and of their reliance upon the web of life for their own survival. There was a reverence for all life and the balance of life, because their very survival depended on learning how to live within this balance.

In modern culture, many have forgotten our interdependence with nature, and therefore we have lost the knowledge of how to maintain right relationship with nature. The call to pilgrimage frequently arises from a deep yearning to reconnect with and activate the innate shamanic wisdom we all possess. At these sacred sites, we receive spiritual downloads, and we are reawakened to that ancient wisdom. We can never return to not knowing what we now feel pulsing in our cellular nature. This knowing ignites a renewal of the heart; it propels us forward to bring this awakened knowledge to the world and to our communities in sacred service to the larger vision of planetary wholeness.

In Africa, for instance, we encounter the planet's oldest known birthplace of humans and most animal species. This motherland's wealth of ancient mythology, religion, shamanic culture and tradition, and human and animal heritage is palpable when you step onto the land. It is also worth remembering that, far back in geologic time, all the Earth's continents were connected as one large landmass called Pangaea. The earliest land species roamed upon this single supercontinent—a deeply unifying experience for our cellular DNA heritage. Like we humans, the Earth herself undergoes change and transformation along a spiral path; therefore we can gain perspective by looking at how she has altered and how our human evolution is tied to hers. When we return to sacred sites from the past, our cells awaken to the energy of these places, and we remember some part of our primal nature.

The supercontinent of Pangaea existed about 200 million years ago, and began to split during the Early Jurassic Epoch, leading to the formation of our modern continents and oceans. This idea, first put forth by German meteorologist Alfred Wegener in 1912, is now better understood through plate tectonics, which demonstrate that the breakup occurred in stages. As it turns out, fascinatingly, Earth has likely seen multiple supercontinents throughout its history. Earth's tectonic plates, which slowly drift across the planet's surface over millions of years, can cause the formation and disintegration of continents. This process is broadly known as the supercontinent cycle. Today's continental movements suggest that a new supercontinent might form in the next 250 million years, as plates collide together once more.

From a shamanic viewpoint, Earth's movement toward a single landmass mirrors humanity's potential to unite as one. The hope is that it won't take millennia for us to recognize our unique contributions and see beyond narrow, self-interested perspectives. By valuing our diversity and working collectively for the greater good, we can foster creativity and ensure a balanced relationship with the planet. This balance requires self-responsibility and respect for nature, moving away from greed, and recognizing that conflict with external groups and individuals often reflects our own internal struggles. In essence, we are unknowingly doing battle with ourselves when we go to battle with others. Our desire to strip the planet of her wealth and resources comes from a misguided belief that we need money and power, because "the other" is always out to harm us. Healing comes from confronting and integrating these shadow aspects within ourselves.

Visiting sacred sites worldwide reconnects us to our shared human lineage, offering insights from nature and our ancestors about improving our collective journey. History's conflicts, fueled by our primal instincts, contrast with our capacity for unity and creativity. These sacred places remind us to harness our diverse talents and collaborate harmoniously, aligning with a global vision for the greater good. They inspire us to activate our innate potential for the benefit of the planet.

Because many sacred sites in the United States are not recognized as such, it became important to me to create a sacred site in the beautiful ancestral mountains where I live, to make a portal, a land altar of Aquarian Elemental Temples, for those seeking healing transformation through Venus Rising's ceremonies and healing programs. Collaborating with Venus Rising's soul friends and family, we have co-created with Mother Earth (aka Gaia, Isis, or Pachu Momma, and the Green Man) a very special sacred site in the magical blue mountains of Western North Carolina, where people can receive healing activations during ceremonies and our Venus Rising programs and initiations, including SHIP. To some degree, the power of the temples and their blessed awakening was made possible by the powerful shamanic activations and ceremonies that I and others have received from our blessed lineage elder teachers, many of whom are in spirit now.

Further possibilities arise from connecting with other sacred places and healers on our pilgrimages around the world and consciously connecting to the equally sacred grid right here in these magical blue mountains on Dove Mountain, with an awakening ceremony for each Elemental Temple.

20

Embodying Shamanic Consciousness and Living a Magical Life

In this book, I have explored and shared my deeply felt sense of how every one of us on this planet can make the journey home to our true self by awakening the Aquarian Shaman within. I have shared with you my perspective on why it is important to embody shamanic consciousness and co-create shamanic relationships. This book has described just a few of many possible outer-world tools: the shaman's medicine chest, ceremony, ritual, and working with sacred spaces and objects that give us a physical connection to spiritual consciousness. I have invited you to connect with the inner-world tools of shamanic consciousness and to inspire your inner soulful child, as your imaginative and playful guide, to engage with elemental and archetypal teachers. We have explored how, once you've activated your inner Aquarian Shaman, you will stimulate the energy fields within and around you to manifest new outer-world experiences and attract other embodied shamanic souls into your sacred circles and communities. Finally, this book has delved into the importance of sacred sites that aid seekers in connecting with a deeper understanding of their shamanic consciousness and humanity's lineage, as well as offering soul recovery at a deeper level, inspiring pilgrims to become agents of planetary service.

To ground these sometimes-lofty experiences in human consciousness, I once again wish to say, let's play like we're shamans—it is the most natural thing in the world. In my generation and until more recently, before cell phones and computers replaced nature, many of us as children had our animal companions, our ancestors in the trees we played beneath, and the clouds with funny faces that we would make up stories about, feeling the warm sun on our skin. We had costumes that emboldened us to step into characters we admired or feared. We had our shamanic toys—sticks, rocks, shells, even the castings of bugs that had shed and renewed their bodies—all meaningful sacred objects along our childhood journey. We played instruments like drums, rattles, and kazoos. We ran barefoot without concern, the original earthing or grounding. We bounced on couches with capes on. We dressed up on Halloween to shape-shift for a day.

Reconnecting with the ancient knowledge of our shamanic forebears and integrating it with the visionary blueprint for the Aquarian age, we reawaken our innate sense of wonder and our creative spirit—things we once knew instinctually, before the weight of adulthood and the bombardment of technology anchored us to the mundane. The Bible says, "Except ye be converted, and become as little children, ye shall not enter into the kingdom of heaven." I hope, through this book, to encourage us all to reclaim our inner child, with the child's awe, and re-enter the world of our imaginations, and then to raise that child up into healthy adulthood so we may all become creative, imaginative, and responsible adult children of God. Renew your connection to the child who knows and lives through curiosity, wonder, creativity, and intuition, but also be able to respond to life as an adult with a mature and wise relationship to self and others. This is the both/and of being an awakened Aquarian Shaman. A wise one knows the importance of allowing old patterns to be dissolved in the waters, to renew and refresh. Such a one also understands the value in composting our life's soil into nutrients where we may plant seeds of love, while tending to the practical, day-to-day steps. Likewise, those with shamanic wisdom are aware of the need to maintain and feed the fires of creation and inspiration, without letting the flames grow out of control.

We can bring these three elements of ourselves playfully and purposefully into our hearts, in the place of alchemical magic, where thoughts, inspiration, and the breath of life unite, fanning the flames of creation and manifestation here on Earth. Let us be "recovering shamans," the once-wounded ones, who can now rise up out of apathy and find compassion and forgiveness for ourselves and others. I hope you will step into a grander vision for yourself and the world, pursuing daily improvements and self-awareness. Be responsible for your emotions, seek amends for harm done, and actively forge solutions. When you come into conflict with another person, protect yourself, establish boundaries, and wish for the other's growth and healing. This approach helps break negative cycles, conserving energy for creativity and positive change.

Embrace life with awareness, and practice self-care to help enrich your contributions to the world. Channel the wisdom and adaptability of your inner child through the shamanic path, allowing curiosity and play to inform your roles in life. Celebrate your unique journey of transformation, accepting yourself and others as we navigate life's cycles. Through this acceptance, we can fully express our creativity and meet our needs while engaging in the sacred work of transformation and integration.

As we all raise our frequencies to the next level, our outmoded activities, people, jobs, or homes will inevitably fall away. There will be a period of recalibration and perhaps confusion, and then new activities, people, jobs, homes, or other creations will emerge from the darkness of the unknown on the sacred spiral path of transformation. In this way, we learn to see through shamanic eyes and a shamanic heart that all our experiences—life, death, and rebirth—are the glorious catalysts that grow us. There is a richness, clarity, and depth in this way of living. The deeper the lows, the more joyous the highs. We learn to dance with life passionately when we have a shaman's alchemical heart, capable of transformation and transmutation, and we have learned to view everything with the eyes and heart of the Aquarian Shaman.

For a time in life, we learn to grow because we don't like the company we keep. By attracting the opposite of what we truly want, we go through the hard lessons and evolve ourselves. Yet when we embody shamanic consciousness we spend far less time operating unconsciously from our shadow nature, we begin to vibrate at a higher frequency and now can enjoy the learning and growth that arise, not so much from chronic suffering, but from like attracting like. Our imaginal cell fields begin to attract one another, and we co-create big, beautiful dreams together through synchronicity. When we find one another and together are committed to co-creating the vision of higher love and wisdom on Earth, we can make a tremendous difference in the world. To quote Margaret Mead, "Never doubt that a small group of thoughtful, committed citizens can change the world; indeed, it's the only thing that ever has." This profound statement certainly reflects my experiences.

So, then, embrace love for God/Goddess/Creator and yourself, letting this love guide your actions and being. When you orient your life toward your passions, and practice love and gratitude for the beauty of life's oneness, your joy becomes magnetic, drawing others toward you. This resonance can build local communities, starting small and expanding to encompass the world. As more people learn to operate as fully embodied Earthlings, infused with the frequencies of higher love and wisdom, the whole world will have the opportunity to evolve and embrace their future selves.

There is a beautiful song by Danya River called "Heart Is Wide Open," which reminds us that if we make room in our hearts for life and love, the whole world can fall in. Danya River shares this about her song on her website: "This track was inspired by a quote by Dr. Kent Keith (often misattributed to Mother Teresa): 'May God break my heart so completely that the whole world falls in.'" Her song is truly a shamanic song, expressing that we grow into our larger being through the cracks and openings in our hearts. Her lyrics state:

Love, I pray that you break
my heart so wide open
that the whole world falls in.
If I'm made for love
make me strong enough.

My prayer is that you, my reader and fellow traveler, will dream a shamanic dream with me and feel inspired to awaken the next octave of your soul's journey, the Aquarian Shaman for a changing world. I encourage you to make use of practices that support you in staying awake and alive! As one who has carried and shared a message of hope for more than forty years, I have seen over and over again that awakened shamanic beings who are committed to putting daily shamanic principles into practice, and channeling shamanic consciousness, can and do change their lives—and I believe this is how the world will meet its true destiny! In closing, I will leave you with this. I have always loved the lyrics of the "Age of Aquarius":

When the moon is in the Seventh House
And Jupiter aligns with Mars
Then peace will guide the planets
And love will steer the stars
This is the dawning of the age of Aquarius
Age of Aquarius . . .
Harmony and understanding
Sympathy and trust abounding
No more falsehoods or derisions
Golden living dreams of visions
Mystic crystal revelation
And the mind's true liberation
Aquarius
Aquarius

Venus Rising Association for Transformation

Shamanic Recovery and Discovery Process

Preamble

The Venus Rising Shamanic Recovery and Discovery Process is grounded in the traditions and principles of all twelve-step fellowships. Our intention is to create a bridge that incorporates the roots of the twelve-step philosophy and expands it to embrace shamanic consciousness. It means walking the shaman's path with daily awareness of our recovery on all levels and discovering our own unique lived expression of shamanic recovery. Recovery from addictions means a willingness to open to the Great Mystery that we have experienced as a void. We have tried to fill the void with all manner of substances and obsessive behaviors. Once we understand we are not alone, what appeared a frightening plunge into the void reveals itself as instead a surrender to the dance with the Great Mystery. Obsession alchemically transforms into passion, and the dance with our inner shamanic power becomes a union with the divine. By facing and embracing the darkness we sought to avoid, we come home to ourselves.

This new Shamanic Recovery and Discovery fellowship intends to help us deal with the whole spectrum of addictions and compulsions and simultaneously access our own inner healer/shaman. We are expanding boundaries and are no longer limited by individual "anonymous" programs. Instead we are creating a form of all-inclusive expression. This is an ongoing, dynamic work in progress, and we invite anyone who feels so inspired to help us create and redefine our unique recovery and discovery perspective.

Twelve Steps of Shamanic Recovery and Discovery

1. We accept that we are powerless over our addictive, compulsive, and codependent patterns of thought and behavior—that in the attempt to fill the void rather than embrace it, our lives have become unmanageable.
2. We come to believe that, within ourselves, we can access a power greater than anything we previously imagined, which can open us to love and nurture us through our path of recovery and discovery.
3. Knowing that unconditional love is our healer, we make a decision to surrender our will and our lives to the care of an inner Greater Power as we understand it.
4. We take a loving and fearless inventory of ourselves.
5. We share our inventory with our Greater Power and another person, without the need for self-recrimination, knowing that in naming our shadow we will open our hearts.
6. We're entirely ready to have our Greater Power remove these inner obstacles, and to give up our need to be perfect.
7. We humbly ask our Greater Power to help us let go of all distractions from the divine that manifest in negative and self-destructive patterns of thought and behavior.
8. We make a list of all the persons we have harmed while attempting to fill the void, and become willing to make amends to them all, forgiving them and ourselves.
9. We make direct amends to those we have harmed, except when doing so would injure them or others. When making direct amends would cause harm, we make amends through a ritual or ceremony that honors the other and ourselves.

10. We continue to take personal inventory daily, as an act of reverence, committing to our personal growth. When we are wrong, we promptly admit it and lovingly accept responsibility for our mistakes. We also admit when our boundaries have been violated, and choose to fearlessly and lovingly tell the truth to free ourselves from the bondage of inauthentic living.

11. Through prayer and meditation, we improve our conscious contact with our inner Greater Power, praying only for knowledge of our Greater Power's will for us, and the love and strength to carry that out in our daily lives by acting from love rather than fear.

12. As a result of these steps, we reach a greater understanding of our true selves and are able to carry the message of recovery and discovery in our daily lives. We may then live the passionate dance of co-creating our lives through the synthesis of our will and the will and wisdom of our inner Divine Spirit.

Adapted from the teachings of Alcoholics Anonymous, Codependents Anonymous, and Humans Anonymous, this expansion of the twelve steps is lovingly offered from the participants and staff of Venus Rising to give hope and strength to anyone looking for soulful sobriety.

As we learn how to live our lives on purpose, we will discover a deeper relationship with the Great Mystery, ourselves, and one another. We will honor our ancestors, both those living and the ones who have passed on. We will learn from their failings as well as their successes. We will seek to consciously embrace our own shadows that we have unwittingly taken on from our childhoods and even our past incarnations. We will work to change those aspects of ourselves and our lives that can be changed, with bravery, empathy, compassion, and determination. We will cultivate humility and opening to the divine both within and without, to help us make the changes we seek to make. We will practice surrendering our old ways of being, and thus we will become teachable.

We will gladly show our gratitude by having compassion, empathy, and genuine concern for those among us who are also seeking to transform their lives, and we will support them where possible.

As we live our lives more fully and move closer to our destined selves, we will discover a newfound freedom beyond our prior dreams and spiritual longings.

We will find we have been set free from many of our fears, anxieties, depressions, and other mental, emotional, spiritual, and sometimes physical problems. This newfound freedom in release from the past depends upon a commitment to living a grounded, spiritually disciplined life, one day at a time, while remembering that all life is a spiral path and therefore we must practice patience, humility, gratitude, healthy boundaries, and generosity of spirit for all. The word "discipline" comes from the Latin *disciplina*, which means "instruction or knowledge," so we are in essence being called to seek knowledge of our highest self.

As we transform ourselves, we will automatically begin to transform the world around us. This is done not from a place of codependency, but through leading by example, raising our own principles and frequencies. Through the laws of attraction, we will embrace both shadow and light, to continue assisting our soulful recovery and shamanic evolution.

May we all experience the grace and magic of recovering parts of ourselves we thought were lost, and discovering new parts that have been waiting for us.

Ultimately, we are descendants from the Cosmos and from Great Mystery itself. It is time to remember our sacred lineage and shamanic birthright, and to embrace the Aquarian Shaman within us all. The future is ours if we choose to transform our past and live fully in the present.

> To all my shamanic Aquarian brothers and sis stars
> We are all related
> We are the ones we have waited for
> In love and service to the All,
>
> STAR WOLF

New Paradigm Aquarian Shamans

Linda Star Wolf &
Nikólaus Star Wolf
Timeless Soulmates dedicated to
walking the Aquarian path of Higher
Love and Wisdom, serving the planet
as co-directors of Venus Rising
Association for Transformation, and
honoring the lineage of the Wolf Clan
Teachings & Blue Star Mysteries

Carley Mattimore & John Malan
Shamanic Facilitators & Co-founders of
Aahara Spiritual Community of Venus Rising

Vera Lopez
Shamanic Minister & Spiritual Group
Leader to Sacred Sites

Grandfather Mowgli
Shamanic Minister, Steward of Oz Farm
Sanctuary, & Owner of Still Point Center
for Healing Arts (Cincinnati)

Tammy Billups
Author, Animal-Human Interspecies
Healer, & Pioneer of Animal-Human
Soul Partnership

Sandy Roberts
Nurse Practitioner, Shamanic Minister,
& Shamanic Breathwork Facilitator

Kelley Eden Moonwolf, D.Min.
Shamanic Breathwork Master
Practitioner, Reiki Master, & Retired
Naturopathic Doctor

Lisa Asvestas (right)
Shamanic Minister, Shamanic Breathwork
Facilitator, & Congregation Leader of Third Eye
Tribe of Venus Rising

Brian Delate
Visionary Actor, Filmmaker, Veteran,
& Creator of a One-Person Show,
Revealing Guardian Angels

Shama Viola
Wisdom Keeper,
Creator of Bral
Talej, & Damanhur
Shamanic Guide

Levi Banner, M.A.
Astrologer, DJ, Music Producer,
Shamanic Breathwork Master
Practitioner, & Venus Rising
Core Staff

Judy Redhawk, Ph.D., D.Min.
Shamanic Breathwork Master Practitioner,
Artist in Residence,
Venus Rising & Venus Rising
University Core Staff

Marsha Bleuwolf, D.S.P.S.
Aquarian Woodstock Shamanic Hippie,
Shamanic Breathwork Facilitator, &
Coordinator of Shamanic 12 Steps

Mariko Heart Wolf, D.Min.
Practitioner of Energy Medicine & Shamanic
Breathwork Master Practitioner

Áróra Helgadóttir
Shamanic Breathwork Master Practitioner,
Yoga Teacher, Aquarian Empowerment
Teacher, & Biomedical Engineer

Kathy Morrison
Shamanic Minister, 30 Questions Guide,
& Shamanic Breathwork
Master Practitioner

Nita Gage, M.A., D.S.P.S.
Hoffman Teacher & Shamanic Breathwork
Facilitator, Esalen Institute Faculty

Tom Blue Wolf
Deep Ecology Artist & Earthkeeper of
Twenty-Year-Old Spirit Lodges in Europe,
Africa, & Turtle Island

Joe Doherty
Psychotherapist, Yogi, Shamanic
Minister, & Psychedelic Guide

Daniel Pinchbeck
Author of Breaking Open The Head and
Quetzalcoatl Returns & Teacher of
Online Seminars

Myrna "Amai" Clarice Munchus
Shamanic Minister, Shamanic
Breathwork Master Practitioner,
Ancestral Wisdom Keeper, Dancer,
Ritualist, & Storyteller

Sara Aljneibi
Artist, Writer, Embodiment &
Intimacy Guide, Shamanic Breathwork
Facilitator, Dance & Therapeutic
Movement Practitioner

Laura Wolf
Priestess to the Wild Feminine, Teacher,
Coach, & Retreat Leader

Wind Daughter
Born an Aquarian with Shaman Eyes and
a Gypsy Soul & Medicine Chief of the
Panther Lodge Bear Tribe
Medicine Society

Elaine Yonge
Shamanic, Tantric, & Somatic Breathwork
Facilitator, London, UK

Nicki Skully
Acquired Shamanic Training from
Journeys to Egypt, Peru, Yucatan,
Australia and Created Shamanic
Transformational Work to Empower
Her Students

Emil Shaker
"Wolf of Egypt"
Shamanic Guide
& Wisdom
Keeper of
Ancient
Egyptian
Mysteries

Wendyne Limber
"Sunwoman Magic Maker" Family
Therapist & Carrier of Crow Medicine
Bag, Soulville Conscious Transformation
Community of Venus Rising

Rev. Stephanie Red Feather, Ph.D.
Divine Feminine Facilitator & Coach, Shamanic
Priestess, Multi-Award-Winning Author

Steven Farmer
World-Renowned Author, Teacher,
Shamanic Practitioner, & Soul Healer

Azra Bertrand, M.D.
Founder of Biomancy University,
Author, Healer, & Mystic

Lee McCormick
Founder/Author of Spirit Recovery
Journeys, Workshops, & Books;
Partner in "The Dreaming House"
in Teotihuacan, Mexico; Innovative Leader
in Creating Mental Health & Addictions
Treatment Programs

HeatherAsh Amara
Best-Selling Author, Firewalk Instructor,
& Shamanic Empowerment Leader

Itzhak Beery
Shamanic Teacher, Healer, Trip Leader, &
Founder/Publisher of Shamanportal.org

Jorge Luis Delgado
Lover of Ancient Wisdom, Quechua–Aymara
Chakaruna & Author

Judith Corvin-Blackburn,
L.C.S.W., D.Min.
Transpersonal Psychotherapist, Shamanic
Minister, & Award-Winning Author

Barbara Vitale
Grandmother Blue Star Author &
Ceremonialist

Steve Bhaerman
Cosmic Comic Swami
Beyondananda, Co-author of
Spontaneous Evolution, & Coined
the Term "The Great Up-Wising"

Michael Brant DeMaria
Sound Healer, Wisdom Teacher,
Recipient of Four Grammy
Nominations, Composer of Six
#1 Albums, a Native American
Music Award Winner, Author
of Five Books and a Number of
Award-Winning Films. You can
learn more about Michael's work
and listen to his album *Gaia* at
www.michaeldemaria.com.

Index

Books of Related Interest

Shamanic Breathwork

Journeying beyond the Limits of the Self

by Linda Star Wolf Ph.D.

Foreword by Nicki Scully

Shamanic Egyptian Astrology

Your Planetary Relationship to the Gods

by Linda Star Wolf Ph.D., and Ruby Falconer

Sacred Medicine of Bee, Butterfly, Earthworm, and Spider

Shamanic Teachers of the Instar Medicine Wheel

by Linda Star Wolf Ph.D., and Anna Cariad-Barrett, DMin

Soul Whispering

The Art of Awakening Shamanic Consciousness

by Linda Star Wolf Ph.D., and Nita Gage, DSPS, MA

Foreword by Richard Rudd

Shamanic Mysteries of Egypt

Awakening the Healing Power of the Heart

by Nicki Scully and Linda Star Wolf

The Anubis Oracle

A Journey into the Shamanic Mysteries of Egypt

by Nicki Scully and Linda Star Wolf

Illustrated by Kris Waldherr

Shamanic Mysteries of Peru

The Heart Wisdom of the High Andes

by Vera Lopez and Linda Star Wolf Ph.D.

Animal Wayshowers

The Lightworkers Ushering In 5D Consciousness

by Tammy Billups

Foreword by Linda Star Wolf Ph.D.

INNER TRADITIONS • BEAR & COMPANY

P.O. Box 388 • Rochester, VT 05767

1-800-246-8648 • www.InnerTraditions.com

Or contact your local bookseller